CONTENTS

ACKNOWLEDGEMENTS

The Crimson Light is expressed through the spirit of: faith, unity, truth, presence, forgiveness, conviction, endurance.

The wondrous gifts of the spirit that helps find wisdom, healing, knowledge, prophesy, language and faith, miracles, and discernment in pursue of finding one's self.

The recognition and celebration of achievements gained through the abondanment of fear and the pursuit of your goals through the constant illumination of the Crimson Light that guides you.

My belated parents and in particular my loving mother who remained devoted to my care, whose nurturing and influence helped shape me by becoming one with myself and all of life.

For all mothers and mothers of mothers, who are yet to find your voices, including others who have offered their voices so that the daughters of the world can also find the courage to speak and honour their truth.

For all fathers, and fathers of fathers, who are hurting and have not learned how to constructively deal with their pain; remember, your gain lies in your legacy as the sons and daughters through whom your light shines in the earth.

My loving son Daniel Nervais who has been and continues to be my inpiration.

My siblings, family, and loyal friends, who have all supported and enriched my life immensely; may the Crimson Light continue to shine on all. Thank you.

Miss Syble James, Julie Blanchard, Cleus Doxon, Ian Lewinson, Gorge Livingston and Nadia John, Dela Lubin, Kem Lubin, Vernesta Nervais, Dilan Simon, Valarie Campbell and Maureen Williams for your kindness and support.

For everyone, and every creature, place, event and institution that has touched my life directly and indirectly, through all of which I have now gained my sense of discovering my separate selves.

FOREWORD

I was at a point in my life when I knew that I had to make changes. I felt as if my life had come to a halt. The familiar feeling of failure had become increasingly hard to bear. I felt hollow inside. It seemed as if all I had was the experience of another broken marriage and an exciting business attempt that never really got off the ground. My expectations of a new life on the tropical island of St. Lucia had, in fact, reflected a blighted dream. The dread that I would be faced with questions from members of the "I told you so" society also triggered the need to find answers for myself. Moreover, I knew that deep inside me, there was a strong, loving, and powerful spirit – in other words, the spirit of Shakti.

I had often felt that my decisions were in my best interest, but I was now coming to the conclusion that I would need to reflect, evaluate, and reconsider how my life had been impacted by the choices I had made. I decided to leave no stone unturned as I examined every facet of my life, even if this meant facing my inner fears and the patterns that have emerged throughout my life. I wanted to break the unhealthy cycle, to take ownership and to express the total fullness and potential of who I really am. This would require me to have a clear vision of where I want to be and the steps that I would need to take for my personal journey of transformation.

As I became mindful of the coincidences around me, I saw that life is neither accidental nor coincidental. Life is what is actually happening whilst you are waiting for what you want to happen. Just check out what is actually happening to you right now, whilst you are waiting for what you want to happen.

It is my intention for you, as my companion, to make this journey one of personal transformation, as we venture under the constant illumination and guidance of the Crimson Light and onto the Bridge to Actualising Self-full Love ensuring to leave no stone unturned.

The Crimson Light

The Crimson Light has been that glow,
always resonating inside you.
It is the glow of light that has held onto
you since the time of your birth.
It is in everything you see, touch and smell,
and in everything you hear,
It is in the gaze of a child's eyes, and in their smiles
Just listen to the sounds all around
You can hear it in their cries, and in the cackling of laughter too;
Though dormant, the Crimson Light is alive in you.

It is in the singing of the birds and even in the gust of the wind
That soothes you on a hot summer's day.
It is in the warmth of the sun upon your
face and even in the raindrops too.
If you will only lift your face to the heavens and surrender,
There you can feel the Crimson Light,
In the melting snowflake as it drops on your face,
And if you listen, you can also hear it in the waves of the ocean.

The Crimson Light is there too in the pages of this book
Unfolding as a red rose in bloom,
And though not always visible, the Crimson
Light is in each breath you take.
Once you begin the journey of self-
awareness, you will safely be guided,
Onto the Bridge of Actualising Self-Full Love with the unveiling
And constant illumination of the Crimson Light
As a burning furnace that resonates inside.
Then, and only then, you will realise that the Crimson Light
Has been within you all along: a pilot, just waiting to be ignited.

CHAPTER ONE

The Allegiance of the CrimsonLight

A seemingly noble man, I thought, a man of public stature and recognition and much influence in the community, has just, to my dismay, buried himself right outside the mortuary. Is this a joke or is he just trying it on, or perhaps I should say trying it in' for size?

Mr. Barack Altidore, the forty-seven-year-old president of the district infirmary Hope for the People (HFTP) and owner of the mortuary Final Destination Resort (FDR), voluntarily descended into the tomb, just like that? Never before have I seen someone literally step into a tomb. Furthermore, I had never seen what I can only describe as a "tombed casket."

That casket seemed very unique. It had a strange device attached to the lid, a sort of mechanism in which to convert it directly into a tomb. As you may very well know, a casket would not allow a man of six feet tall to stoop inside it but would only allow him to lie in it (of course, provided that the tomb was long enough). That is how I knew that with one step in, and it was as though Mr. Altidore had been siphoned, *Zoooooooooop*, all the way, straight down.

On one hand, I immediately felt that I understood what I had just witnessed, as if I was there to act out a part of a freaky Stephen King movie. On the other hand, I felt that there was a greater significance to my presence, but it was not clear what that was. A minute's delay would have made all the difference.

Why am I here? I thought. I had previously asked myself this several times, accompanied by the voice of spiritual teacher Deepak Chopra, who assists many individuals in finding their life's purpose. Why are you here? The answer, "I am here to be of service to others," was, perhaps, one borrowed from Iyanla Vanzant, who is famously known for helping people fix their lives on the OWN television network. You see, sometimes in our quest for answers, we borrow that which seems nice, fitting, or appropriate, just to fill in the gap at that moment.

Now, I had learned that since I was given so many seemingly unhealthy ideas, and some healthy ones too, I thought it wouldn't hurt to at least borrow a few. Especially those that I felt could serve me well, such as Iyanla's response regarding her own life's purpose. Moreover, I am always conscious of the fact that I never have to worry about returning them or paying them back. I have also learnt that people are generally very generous in giving ideas and are equally open to take or even steal other people's ideas too, whether they are good or bad, but they make them their own, anyway.

Somehow, being of service to others, with the spiritual connotation that I had long envisioned, did not seem fitting for witnessing Mr. Barack Altidore's departure. I really couldn't see how I could be of service to the man, whom I could only presume was no more. I remembered that there could be several reasons why we are witnesses to something or someone. For example, it could be to learn something, to achieve something, or perhaps to relate to others what we have seen. Also, as you might have experienced on many occasions, someone voluntarily giving you just the information you needed and exactly at the right time, too.

Having said that, I believe that some people are just information collectors; the more they get, the more they collect. In many cases, they are not too bothered whether it seems useful or not at the time, but they collect anyway. They are the type of people who say, "I'll have that, just in case."

Whatever the cause, I was totally convinced that there was a good reason for my presence, seeing Mr. Altidore stepping into the tombed casket. Although I must admit that on several occasions, I did fantasise about wanting to see such a thing. However, the desire for self-awareness and spiritual attainment left me with little room to dwell on this kind of thinking. Then again, perhaps Hollywood has surpassed satisfying my appetite.

At that time, I was curious about how I would react to witnessing a tragedy. But the weaning of that curiosity has since left me feeling rather blessed, simply because I have been spared the potential condition of post-traumatic stress disorder (PTSD) or other forms of severe depression, as a cause. Could it be, however, that fantasy had become so embedded in my unconsciousness and was now re-emerging into my consciousness? Those were the thoughts going through my mind.

"Why am I here?" I could hear a whisper in my ear. "There are no accidents and no coincidences. Remember this! Nothing happens by chance but by *choice*. Nothing!"

Though I accepted this truth, that accidents and coincidences are ways in which we attract experiences that shape us, I still found it hard to accept this reality: the reality that being a witness to seeing Mr. Altidore stepping into the tombed-casket just like that was indeed a choice I really made.

As you might have guessed by now, I switched my attention into the common mode of defense: "No! I would not choose to witness what I could only presume to be a suicide. That's crazy!" Even though I had gotten close to that point myself, to making my own exit. Well, mine would not have been a tombed casket, of course, but I mean, the passing of the last breath. Still, I do admit, even then, it was a crazy idea.

"Such a choice has to be of a sick mind, don't you think?" the voice spouted. "And if that were true, would it not mean that a *sick* mind and a *healed* mind are just flip sides of the same coin?"

Yeah, but who would want to witness a suicide? I thought.

The voice uttered in my head, "The answer to your question lies within. Remember, truth is never really far away from the seeker, which means the seeker is also the finder; just flip sides of the same coin. Therefore, be mindful of exactly what it is that you seek, for those who seek shall surely find."

"Why would I want to make a choice to witness a suicide?" I responded.

"Ah, I see! Now you are asking the question in the specific way which would identify the answer to the question that you seek. By that I mean, there are set principles of order for everything and every condition in this life. It all depends on the desired outcome of your action and intention. Therefore, they can be applied accordingly."

Then, I thought, *Principles of order? As if life is not complicated enough. Plus, I still have issues discerning right and wrong, and now giving me set principles of order to think about?*

However, not wanting to implicate the matter at hand, I decided not to dwell on this point much longer.

The voice continued, "Therefore, it is important to know how to address the questions to the answers that you seek; for instance, 'why' implies reason, of cause and effect: the cause being the response to an action, and effect is the impact of the response, of an action. For this reason, you cannot separate the two, for where one is found, there too you shall find the other. To deal with the cause, you must examine the effect, and likewise, to deal with the effect, you must examine the cause. Now, this is the basic root of any matter and thus serves as the flip side of the same coin: for there is no good without bad and no cold without hot. Neither will you find top without bottom;

likewise, would white ever exist without black? Moreover, you must know that even life and death are just a breath; one given, the other taken away, just two sides of the same coin."

The analogy of the coin had got me thinking about money, which also shed some light on why it was difficult to just bypass this point. Could I ever recondition my mind, to disassociate the effect of money on various areas of my life, that it does not have to be at the forefront? However, as a good student, I reminded myself of this practice of awareness, that "there are no accidents and no coincidences, but the choices that we make." I decided to consciously encode in my mind the flip sides of the coin, and then, I resolved to recite a few in my head: to learn or teach; to mourn or dance; to bless or curse; to sing or cry; to sigh or smile; to fight or unite; to feel or heal; to hold on or release. *All of these I had done and observed on my journey of self-awareness and enlightenment,* I thought to myself.

Still, "Why am I here?" I kept asking myself over and over. Then I became aware, as though the soft voice in my head would voluntarily choose to respond, whether I verbalised my thoughts or simply kept them in my head.

"Remember," the voice continued, "as you said, to make a choice to observe such an act, as you have, is the behaviour of a sick mind, and this is also true: that you are not here by chance, but by choice."

"Do you mean that I have a sick mind?" I asked.

"Those were your words! Is it not said that it is from the abundance of the heart that the mouth speaks?"

The fact that I had caught myself thinking, *I don't like the word "sick," because it actually makes me feel bad, and I like the word "healed," because it makes me feel good,* made me aware that I had not fully, if at all, accepted the flip side of the coin.

"Are you saying that we cannot use one side without the other?" I asked.

"That's right! But 'consider' is perhaps more appropriate in this context. For good would not exist without bad; since we live in a world of opposites."

This understanding gave me an insight that maybe I had been there to learn something about the state of my mind. However, I got comfort in believing that if I was there to learn, I would also have something to teach. Therefore, if it's about death, well, there would be something of the opposite: life. On the other hand, could this mean that I was so sick and in need of the infirmary?

Somehow, I found comfort whilst in dialogue with the voice that convinced me that there is something to learn here. Immediately, that conclusion reminded me that sometimes, all there is to really learn from dialogue is best not to engage in it. After all, we can't go on paying attention to everything we hear or think of; otherwise, we'd go cuckoo.

According to your belief be it onto you.

As I continued to ponder on Mr. Altidore's departure, I thought, *But it's not every day that you see this kind of thing: someone stepping into a tombed casket just like that.*

Then, the soft voice was again audible: "Yes and no. This is not something that you see every day; and yet it is. In any case, how can you expect to see what is happening in the east if you are facing the west, or what is happening above, if your attention is below? Even commoner, you may find yourself staring at something but you do not see it, because you are not clear of your intention, whilst your attention becomes distorted. Hence, the proverb "They have eyes yet they do not see, ears yet they do not hear." Think of it this way: "Attention is the lover always seeking to be loved by intention, regardless of whatever state he finds her in."

"Does the mere absence of your sight and awareness add meaning for whatever activity is taking place around you?" the voice continued.

"Therefore, does not the fundamental cause of your knowing lie in the meaning you impress upon a thing? But be warned! Even your inactiveness is not without meaning, because your decision to not actively do something still entails doing something about nothing. It is like dropping a pebble into a pond; whether you observe the ripple effect or not, it still happens. And the effect can only be experienced according to your attention and perception of it. Now, whether it is that initial drop, or the extent of the ripple of waters, that disappears into infinity, it all depends on what you choose to make of it."

I was still left a little confused but "coin-logically" speaking, something seemed clear. I understood one thing: that it was up to me to make head or tail from what I had seen that morning when Mr. Altidore stepped into the tombed casket, just like that. For this reason, I accepted the viewpoint that I was at liberty to delve as far as I wished for meaning of that experience. I had the power to make it or change it any which way I wanted by simply impressing whatever meaning I would choose to impart, and that would determine my experience.

Things seemed to be getting clearer as I was reminded: *To yourself be true.*

My overall intention, to experience something enriching to my life, seemed easy. I thought, *All I need to do is, simply, hold the picture of the outcome in my mind's eye as though ready to put on canvas.* However, I also became aware that the ripple effect of my intention also offered an increased responsibility for whatever action I would take. As I reflected on the flip side of the coin, I also became aware that I could not change what I had observed. In any case, I had tried doing that in past times, which had become a pattern of denying what I had truly seen, heard, touched, smelt, or felt. It was as though I learnt to perpetually doubt my senses altogether over time. It seemed like acceptance was never part of the equation, thus leaving me often confused, and as a result, I am still continuing my course in Sensory Connectivity.

I got the impression that my real power lay only in the change of my perception. It seemed that, to change my perception of the picture requires that I take the time to look deep, and looking deep demands my attention not only to create, but also to eradicate the undesirable things from my mind.

I was graduating from the secondary level of taking ownership of my life and learning to trust my senses once more; after all, they must have been given to me for a good purpose.

Drawing on Paul McKenna's teachings gave me courage; he said that sometimes we need to have frequent exposure to something before we can confidently handle it. Consequently, I adopted the idea that perhaps the scenario regarding Mr. Altidore had presented itself as a form of boot camp, a sort of training field that would allow me all the familiarity necessary. This time, I would not be wondering, What if I had gone as intended? Applying changes had become like ending an unhealthy relationship. You know you should dissolve it, but weeks and months, even years go by, and you are still there, deep in it. Later down the road, you think to yourself, *I could have been over this by now*, but you allowed yourself to be hunted by the potential pain, guilt, and shame, forgetting what you stand to gain. This had been my realisation.

Nevertheless, I felt that my observation of the event of the dawn was offering me new meaning for my life. Though I had done the math, I still allowed the income state of ambivalence for a while. It might have been the tiresome state of that feeling in itself that helped me to get in touch with my feelings as advocates of emotions, such as Gary Zucav recommended; I became mindful that my feelings of confusion seemed to have provided me a sense of delayed reaction and anticipation, for what, I was not certain about.

My purpose and why I was there: I was slowly accepting that perhaps I had unconsciously made that choice to be there; to see Mr. Altidore descending into the tombed casket, just like that. Strange as it may seem, I sensed safety in this confusion, for at least to provide myself an element of expectation. In my mind, that expectation would ensure me of a purpose. You see, sometimes we miss the subtle transformation because we become so accustomed to working with confusion and drama. As far as I was concerned, this confusion would somehow act as a bridge of filling in the gap. By that, I thought, I also voided the risk of jumping into any kind of conclusion. Then I thought, this is a real classic example of the mind games we play, though a revelation in itself, through which I felt that I was on the other side of the coin, of the peace that I was seeking.

So I affirmed Louise L. Hay's teachings, that "everything I needed to know, I would know at the right time, space, and sequence." I only needed to flip sides, intermittently, and I would be alright, as she also reminds you to be patient and gentle with yourself. *I know, patience and gentleness do not mean deliberate implications of confusions of course, but all these are part of the process*, I told myself.

My commitment to know and to understand exactly why I was there, as a witness, substantiated my desire to apply myself whilst in the Open University of Life: to be receptive and to learn whatever I felt was necessary. By so doing, I would avoid repeating the same lessons over and over again, as I had done several times in the past. By that, I certainly would not be witnessing this kind of scenario again. I was confident that I would achieve my goal, because I felt that I was now outgrowing the old cloak given to me in my youth, a cloak that had labelled Stubbornness" and "Hard-Headedness" inside. I was now ready to be cloaked in my new garments that were labeled "Steadfastness" and "Level-Headedness," manufactured by the Crimson Light, with care Instructions: ability to withstand all temperatures and conducive to all climates, with an unlimited warranty. Perhaps it was a fake, but nonetheless, this cloak would aid me in my attainment of personal growth, peace, joy, and prosperity. It felt right. You see, I had become conscious about names that I carried, particularly around my throat chakra. I was now ready to keep my airways clear, to freely ask specific questions as I wished, like "Why am I here? What did I see? What did I hear? What did I feel? What did I smell? What did I touch? What did I taste?" Even then, the answers seemed to be floating at the top of my head, yet they proved unclear.

I had bombarded my mind with questions, as if trying to allure some visualization technique, as though I was on one of Paul McKenna's programs: Change Your Life in Seven Days, but at the core of it all, I just wanted to know why I was there. I felt that there was a message there for me. Then the voice, which was no longer soft but instead this time had thundered, "Be still and know that I am the Crimson Light!"

Being still it is not easy, I thought. However, I had learned to anchor on; the fact that something is not easy to apply does not, itself, make it impossible to happen. It took me many years to grasp stillness because of my want for quick answers and solutions, including my incoherent questions. In conjunction with the meditative state that I had previously experienced, I had come to understand that to be still is not being perturbed or restless, but rather to be restfull in faith that all is well, once you have done all that you possibly can. To help me direct my focus on stillness, I immediately remembered the countless times of searching for a name or an object, and seemingly without effort, it would show up. This often happens just after giving up on the very thing or of being still. Perhaps you've experienced that too. This, however, led me to conclude that whilst stillness acts as a highway by which information flows, I feel that my lifetime endeavour would be toward mastering stillness. Often, when I think I have got it, something like Mr. Altidore's departure would come along and throw me right off track again. In turn, this would often lead me back to square one, wondering what happened and to re-embark on learning to be still again.

It is often in such situations that I tend to make a conscious effort to remember the effect of the pebble thrown in the pond. I would remind myself, even though it seems like I have come around full circle, nevertheless, I have travelled, and therefore, there is no journey without something to experience and learn. It may even mean to collect information that I could pass on to someone or to even pride myself in discovering the quickest and longest route to full circle.

Now, despite not being able to make complete sense of what I had witnessed that day, one thing I was certain about is that I could clearly *see* the hole. Even though I was standing on the opposite side of the road, I could somehow, unquestionably, without a doubt see it. Though not with my naked eyes, but somehow, I could see the hole that Mr. Barack Altidore had stepped into, just like that. It was a black hole. A seemingly bottomless, smoky black hole, really.

Pardon me if I sound confused or even amazed, but I felt that a warm presence had enveloped my being-ness; even then, I was experiencing a presence unlike any other. It was like an assurance, as though I was actualising love by just being there, in that specific moment. There was meaning to my presence, which had felt neither good or bad; it just was. I had learned from all the great teachers, however, that the presence I felt was a form of love. I had caught myself wondering, But love from whom? And for what? Was it for Mr. Altidore? Or his assistant Harry, whom I vaguely knew, or perhaps Christian, the other observer, who happened to be my former manager and ex-lover, or was everyone experiencing what I felt? Was it my mind at play? I had no idea, but it felt like the warmest glow, with a much higher intelligence, was orchestrating the whole event of the dawn. Nevertheless, I was beginning to relax in stillness.

The repetition of questions resonated as though it were the constant ringing of a song that had played over and over, and was still echoing in my head: "Why am I here?" Despite the fact I felt lost, I knew that I was free. I felt scared, yet safe; elated, but saddened and strange, yet very familiar, all at the same time, whilst the allegiance of irresistibly brilliant rays of the Crimson Light was literally hovering just above me.

Despite all else, that presence, though intensely felt, was easier to accept than the descent. Perhaps it's because I had experienced bouts of this magnetic force before and was increasingly becoming more aware of its nature. For example, unknown to him, my supervisor at the University of East London taught me something about presence. I walked into his office one day. As I recall, I had failed my written papers with what I think looked like a double "FF." Until then, I didn't know that that grade existed. I mumbled something to him, but the old cloak I wore that was labelled "lacking self-confidence" had actually blocked my throat. I could not find my voice to express what I wanted to say. However, I left his office feeling quite blissful. I had left with something far more valuable than if it had been "AA" (providing that exists at all). Some years later, however, looking into Dr. John Dermatini's eyes, in one of his London seminars, also taught me something about presence no one can deny. So I intentionally allowed my feet to carry me because I wanted to shake his hand. Now, although my old cloak was wearing off, I still felt challenged, and right there and then, I had to make an oath:

Mr. Pain! What do you want of me?
Why bother me now, more than ever?
So much I have done to keep you happy inside; so much!
Mr. Pain, no more can I afford to keep you in here.
You have outgrown this garment that you now struggle to wear.
Look! The threads have been pulled apart
And your seams are now busted on all sides.

Mr. Pain, you may no longer reign
For surely, even you, too, can see

That the patches and darns, though they may be in style,
But certainly not for those who know that you can no longer hide,
Even from bright colours of distortions
That constantly seeks out attention.

Mr. Pain, as you well know, time is important,
So don't you waste yours nor mine.
Therefore, I now permit you to be released,
Be transformed, for ultimately, that is what you must do.
Return unto self and be joyous,
For that is where it is promised we'll surely meet again.

Then, I permitted myself to speak. I said, "Thank you. But I must say, your eyes are beautiful." They were most dazzling to my eyes as they transmitted a sense of grace directly to my soul. Though often indescribable, I recognise the essence of presence almost everywhere. This is how I knew that it was the Crimson Light that had glowed upon me, which seemed to perfectly reflect the words of my teacher Emmet Fox, in his essay on faith.

Fox said, "Nothing can come into your experience unless it first enters your mentality and nothing can enter your mentality unless it there finds something like itself to which it can attach itself to."

This teaching has increased my understanding of how it might *feel* to recognise the allegiance of the Crimson Light to accomplish my desire. Yet I struggled to refrain from thinking that my ego might take over and cause me to become swell-headed. And so could I ever accept that something as wonderful as the light that had hovered over me would find something like itself in my mentality to which it can attach to? And if so, could I also accept that I am that which is …?

I was challenged, by my sense of worth, to think that the Crimson Light had hovered over me; a thought too wonderful to fathom and to acknowledge my experience. Aha! There was comfort in knowing that the warm glow had, indeed, found something like itself inside me, and the truth that I was seeking, that there had to be a significant purpose of my presence of witnessing Mr. Barrack's descent. And that purpose, in turn, had also found something like itself in me, on which it could attach itself to. I was accepting the essence of both sides of the coin, that this realisation would serve as my point of reference to establishing my position. Now, it is often said that, "To know where you are going is to know where you've been and where you are." Basically, you have to do the maths. With that in mind, I knew that there was no way that I could have witnessed without having the need to testify: I just didn't know how it would manifest.

The modes of flipping in and out of consciousness seemed more like lucid dreaming. As if I were confused one minute and would happily be directing my dreams the next. Yes! The voice began to make sense. I realised that I could actually choose the tone and colour of the mood, of exactly what I wanted to prophesy into my life. It would be as if I was really acting in a movie. Then I reaffirmed in my mind that it is not what happens to you that matters, but it is what you do about what happens; that is what truly matters. Why am I here? The answer to this question would unfold in many different ways in my head and would demand an action that would determine the outcome.

The realisation that I could act as though I were a movie star was a powerful and exciting idea that led me to understand the mode of pursuit that I should take, which meant I could also have fun. I also knew from experience that things can change, just as though another pebble had been dropped into the pond, thus causing another ripple effect. The voice reminded me that sometimes, it's best to remain totally open to new experiences by not imposing limiting expectations of the past. Whilst the past presents certain benefits, like developing and increasing our confidence, by which we tend to gauge our competencies, I was now willing to take a different angle this time. I wanted to put my mind-movie to the test and to operate from a place of no limitation, because according to the good word, "Whatever you sow is what you reap."

Furthermore, to achieve something so grand and miraculous would leave me with no doubt that I had touched new dimensions. For this reason, I felt it would also serve me well to adopt a flexible approach, especially in consideration that if I were indeed an actor, then there must be a director, for where one is found, there too you shall find the other. I was ready to be directed and to follow instructions, even though I often prefer to just do my own thing and even take the initiative at times. Nevertheless, I had learned, where two shall agree upon a thing, it shall be done, through the power of the Crimson Light.

What would I need to be doing or have to make this happen? What would I want to take away from this experience? I wondered. I want to be at liberty to express my creativity and to operate from a deep sense of self-awareness so as to understand what stuff I am made of. Especially since I no longer believe myself to be a liability but rather an asset to the human race. This would allow the opportunity to find out for myself what it means to be made in God's image and likeness and the universal power of intention, which always operates for the highest good of all concerned.

Now, instinctively, I knew that the director was clearly the Crimson Light, because revelation is light. My mind-movies had been rolling in preparation, for the movie *A Bridge to Actualizing Self-Full Love* was being filmed.

Not surprisingly, I was experiencing a degree of nervousness and of being scared, because all the miracles in my life seemed to have manifested at a cost; well, that is, with the exception of the best gift, of course: the gift of breath. Although I am not at all certain that breath is cost-free, since it bears a responsibility to maintain its quality, accordingly.

On one hand, I thought I should adapt the omission of any estimation of cost; simply, for fear it would be too much, and I would miss out on the many wonderful miracles in my life. Now I am not sure exactly what this journey entails, in terms of cost, but according to Jesus Christ, to enter the kingdom, you must be like a child. So the idea to count the cost is perhaps not the best attitude for now; after all, children don't go around with calculators, making estimations for explorations. They just explore. However, my idea to omit the question is not without cost, since I had been cautioned that there is system of order for all things. Now I am bound to flip sides.

The Holy Bible also states, "Which man builds a house and does not count the cost?" Does it mean that I am a coward to not consider cost? If one should ask, "What am I prepared to give up for being a star and for getting onto the Bridge of Actualising Self-full Love?" what would my answer be? The answer would be clear: my all, and all that I am, and all that I have – my humility, my pride, my soul.

The consolidation of my reasoning gave me a sense of inner peace. As though in acknowledgement to that which I had concluded was the gentle voice with a sweet whisper, "Keep on keeping on, my child."

Now, those words had never failed me, because they carry a stamp of integrity and courage, but they also possess a warning that could take one beyond the grave. Nevertheless, the taste of the warm glow that hovered around me had made me desire for more. Therefore, I would not turn back, because the Crimson Light had given me sweetness. In this case, you could say it was not greed, but it just yielded.

Now, according to Lisa Nichols, you've got to be intentional. So here I am, an actor, my secret passion. I will now run with it. I will hold nothing back. I will now allow the creative force to express the part which I am to act. I am now trusting that somehow, the gods had trained me to perform this act, to the best of my ability.

Where there is no vision, there is no mission; therefore, the people perish. No, I will not perish. The mind-movie of my secret passion would not allow me to perish. Instead, it was stirring a vision of the Bridge of Actualising Self-full Love, in my mentality that I began to rehearse immediately. I will make it happen. *Even though the dimensions of the bridge were not clear, since I had intended operating on an unlimited sphere, who cares?* I thought. I will just allow my mind to go wild. All I knew was that I had never before seen or experienced anything like it.

It could have been the effect of the light that caused the vision to seem so bright, after a while, that a burning desire was sown, which left me in full anticipation of its manifestation.

As my heart thumped, I could not help but think, *Oh, sweet love, abundance of love, but how is that to be, with Mr. Barack Altidore stepping into the tom bed-casket just like that?*

Therefore, I have only to rely on the universal laws that govern the allegiance of the Crimson Light to guide me.

Anchoring Points

There are no accidents and no coincidences, but the choices
we make. Today, I am making a choice to trust my
- intentions,
- pace, and
- intuitions.

I am now open and receptive to the guidance of the Crimson
Light; therefore, I am trusting the choice I have made to
- observe,
- listen, and
- act.

The Allegiance of the Crimson Light

The allegiance of the Crimson Light never fails,
Though not always apparent.
Its glow, you may not always see it to follow,
But like a river, sometimes shallow,
And other times so intense that
Its maddening passion would break its banks,
And after you have been tossed from side to side,
Not knowing whether you landed on the left or the right,
Then you realise that you just can't hide the evidence of the ride
That you took on the tide of the Crimson Light.
That is how you know you are indeed a part of the Crimson Light.

CHAPTER TWO

The Desire of the Crimson Light

Everyone and everything seemed to be positioned so orderly, including the row of buildings; the mortuary, Final Destination Resort (FDR); the infirmary, Hope for the People (HFTP); and Grazebrook Primary School (GPS), with the exception of the pet-food warehouse, of course, which was located directly across from the school, at the end of the dead-end street. They conveyed the sense as though they had been imposed on sacred ground, surrounded by the greenest cornfield that I had ever seen. The cornfield, too, had been planted in perfect rows and could hardly have gone unnoticed, as the stalks harmoniously waved their blooming heads, synchronising with the light breeze that blew. I got a sense as though they were all strategically placed, in a purposeful and ceremonial manner, each stalk, in competition, seeking for my attention. Naturally, it was the perfect dance.

The air glittered and appeared crystal light. Each man seemed relaxed in his role. Christian, standing discreetly at the opposite end of the infirmary, observed the event of the dawn. As though ensuring everything goes to plan, Harry stood in full view, with his back against the doorway of the mortuary. To his right was the infirmary, and to his left was the school. His fiery crimson shirt, which was contrasted against his stone gray pants, made him even more noticeable. Now, since we were all wearing gray, although in varying degrees, this drew my attention towards an incomprehensible yet evident consensus: why we were there. Each witness's eyes seemed to have derived from an exact point of a right angle. Their rays, pairing and gazing, as Mr. Barack Altidore appeared to be striding effortlessly and with admirable precision, I dare say. He was elegantly dressed, in a brilliant white linen suit. Contrasted by a slash of gray across his shirt collar and a bright purple flower neatly tucked into the buttonhole of his left lapel, Mr. Altidore looked sharp. His sombre facial expression was enough to get the impression that a grand finale was about to take place. Only a few yards to go before he would attempt to open the lid of the tombed casket.

However, it seemed like the frequent intervals of consciousness had hijacked my neurological pathways, as each left me with the burning question in mind: Why am I here? Only to be reinforced by the fact that I was becoming more convinced that there is something to be learned from everything. And this led me to believe that I was experiencing what Stuart Wilde meant in *33 Steps to Reclaiming Your Inner Power*. Wilde explained that the process of finding your infinite self can seem like a *dance* of confusion and certainty; that is, until you are able to completely focus on achieving your desires. It is about finding your feet, so to speak. He also said that the desire of a person is what the soul seeks, and that, in turn, constitutes the process by which wishes and conditions counteract with each other. Consequently, that was where I was at, but with the exception that my dance seemed more like a quickstep tango, instead of a slow-paced waltz. Clearly, I had not mastered the art of balance of my dance and risked falling flat on my face.

Having procrastinated on the subject, I felt like one in detention, where I knew that I had been given the opportunity to pay attention and to consider the set principles of order for my case. *Perhaps I can take the view that it simply means the steps and procedures required to get onto the Bridge of Actualising Self-full Love*, I thought. Somewhat like what had been applied to nurture and cultivate such a lovely green and healthy cornfield, like the one I had seen near HFTP. I don't think it would have showed up otherwise, which encouraged me to ensure my resourcefulness and to find the right steps and procedures necessary, from whatever was available.

I had previously listened to some of Hollywood's best actors who had emulated others, in order to familiarise themselves with the role they had to act, for creating exactly what they were visualising and to make their end goal more tangible. Conversely, the actor who works with little information is therefore likely to perform his part poorly. With this in mind, I decided the first step on my quest would be to prepare well.

Prepare thy works without and make it fit for thyself in the field and then build, just kept popping up in mymind, as though compelling my attention. I could not, however, claim to understand what that meant. Since it sounded right, I anchored onto what I felt was a basic message that I should ensure to be mentally, physically, and spiritually prepared for my journey. I would take stock and dispatch whatever was required to achieve my goal. In turn, I would gain a sense self-full love. Not just self-love or the innate needs for safety and attachment and so on but rather to fulfill my need for self-actualisation, as described in Maslow's Hierarchy of Needs model. This would require me to gain a deeper sense of my life by raising my consciousness. In other words, why am I here, and how can I learn to honour the purpose of my existence? I hoped that my focus for self-assessment would hold the answers to all my concerns. For me, this was a very hopeful stance, and I would know exactly the role I am meant to act.

I was acknowledging the fact that whenever we are about to operate from a new dimension, we often become uncertain and even, at times, afraid of what we might discover: the unknown, which is often based on fear of past experiences. Perhaps that is why it is said that fear is the beginning of wisdom. Regardless of the fact that I was looking forward to the adventures of my journey, it also felt as though fear had showed up like a bout of motion sickness. Then, I remembered what worked for me in the past about sickness and wanting to be healed. I had learned, according to Louise Hay, that it is important to acknowledge and appreciate "sickness" as a stop sign. Mine had become traffic lights on red that demanded a halt, but still, I was faced with the same question that would validate my position: Why am I here?

I am here to serve, I told myself, and this was my best answer for now. *I could learn how to heal myself, and perhaps teach what I know, and be of service to others.*

This inner dialogue felt right. On reflection, I realised, whether we are aware or not, that is exactly what we do each day in our places of work, or homes, or at play. It is not difficult to see how we serve others. For example, even if you were considered disabled and totally reliant on others for all your basic needs, you are still providing a service. You are providing the other not only with an income, as in many cases, but also information of what it is like to be disabled and how to be caring or compassionate. Furthermore, you could also be offering someone an opportunity of self-introspection. Often, that is how many discover their physical, mental, and spiritual abilities and disabilities, including others like myself, who appear as able-bodied. Now, how profound is that?

In light of this, perhaps the answer to my question ought to be "a giver and recipient of services or a follower and a leader," because, according to the voice, for where there is one, there too, you shall find the other, just flip sides of the same coin. *That means*, I thought, *if I am here to learn, I am also here to teach, and if I am here to be healed, it simply means that I am definitely sick; and perhaps, I would need the infirmary after all.* Therefore, I affirmed my intention to obey the stoplight while anticipating it change to green.

Dear Crimson Light

I am open and receptive to total healing in my life. Amen!

Am I profoundly sick? Or have I driven my mind under the state of mental arrest through the constant questions? Where do I begin?

The soft voice resurfaced: "Sometimes you just have to work with whatever you have."

I had learnt that this attitude can mean a clear demonstration of one's commitment to attaining his goal, and as he perseveres, the universe provides his needs, accordingly. For instance, a few days ago, I felt a little intimidated with my garden project but decided to carry on with the "do it myself" scheme anyway. Just over twenty minutes into the work, my friend Brian, from another district of the island, paid me a surprise visit and took right over from me. Subsequently, I accomplished a great deal more than I had initially intended. All I needed was to start.

Somehow, I could not help but wonder, perhaps that's exactly what Mr. Altidore had done: a "do it myself" by stepping into the tombed casket, just like that. If so, was it just as a means to an end? Or the continuation of his existence in another realm? Whatever his reason, he'd made a start, and that was that. So it made sense to work with whatever I had. For sure, I had gained qualities of courage and determination through facing major life-changing decisions and the acknowledgement of my weaknesses, too: a tendency to be over-optimistic and overly generous. However, I had enough to begin with.

The trick was a shortcut, to charge myself on a "feel good factor" to get motivated. In this case, however, I felt as though I needed everything possible to propel me onto my quest. Such as my new mind-movies backpacked by the reflections of past achievements, so as to consolidate my will to accomplish my goal.

As it happened, I had recently gained a great sense of success through overcoming my fear of various insects, including creepy crawlies, on the island of St. Lucia. They included centipedes, African snails, and roaches, just to name a few. On encountering them, I swear that their eyes would pierce my soul. After quickly weighing my options, I saw that I could make a choice to continue existing with my phobias and never allow myself to experience the freedom that many islanders do. On the other hand, I could face the fear and look forward to the day I would feel free, even on encountering them alone. I also realised that each bout of fear was actually presenting me with the chance to develop my emotional and spiritual immunity. After each successful trial, I would feel increasingly stronger and better about myself, which also allowed me to voluntarily deal with other emotional issues. You could say that the process had become like muscle building. I got the sense that the universe was faithfully providing me an external representation to hinge to, as part of accepting my sickness and need for healing, at the time. As to how much healing I needed? I couldn't tell. I only knew that I had become aware, that within me was the domain where all sorts had crept in.

I had taken on the advice of Susan Jeffers: Decluttering your home is always a good start to decluttering your mind. I allowed myself to be submerged in the evidence of the good feeling that I had previously achieved, so that activity had, in turn, become an anchor.

That day, as I enthusiastically engaged in clearing out my shed, I discovered a lot of cockroaches had made their home in my foot-spa. For a while, I thought I was handling the situation pretty well. That was, until I saw what seemed like hundreds of creatures, just coming out from the base and going off in all directions. Well, on that sight, I am not ashamed to say, I screamed and bawled out loud. However, as the Crimson Light would have it, there were not just one, but two witnesses turned compassionate helpers. I needed help. Even then, I knew in my heart that I had been presented an opportunity for healing myself, so I kept my mind on the benefit and tried to endure the frightening process. I felt that what I was experiencing was very symbolic for all the awful stuff that had crept up inside of me. It had been all those unhealthy experiences that were actually coming out, thus permitting me to look at them for what they were. I had stopped and was paying attention.

As though deliberately charging myself with the "feel good" factor (though I cannot say that I was consciously feeling nice at the time), I continued to project the image of how good I would feel once I had finished dealing with them. That was another anchor.

Consequently, I took comfort in the words so often echoed: "Where there is no pain, there is no gain." With each bout of pain, I would consciously think of a "gain" and then I'd feel good, yes, even about pain. I subsequently developed a stamped signature: *"A-gain for my pain."*

On top of that, I felt that the foot-spa, in particular, was also indicative of my willingness not only to look but to become aware that a new path was opening up before me. I became conscious that I was making my own meaning of what was important to me, just like my endeavour to make sense of why I was there to see Mr. Altidore stepping into the tombed casket, just like that. At the time, I became concerned whether some of the bugs had returned in the shed. The majority of them, thank God, had gone with the pang of the passing of their last breath. This was not too difficult on my part, since I was still at a primary level in the course of having reverence for all forms of life (I am not sure how I would have dealt with them otherwise).

> I am a thinker that creates the thoughts that creates the things.
>
> – Dr. Johnnie Coleman

Now, although I had thoroughly washed and sterilised the foot spa, I knew that I had to get over the idea that those cockroaches had any real power over me. Subsequently, I topped up myself with the feel good factor to keep me going, "a-gain." That, no doubt, entailed the process of making a conscious choice of what lasting effect I wanted to achieve from that experience. As I wondered about the creatures that I thought might have returned into the shed, I realised my creative mind had taken me through some extreme avenues. I saw that, just as the shed had consisted of various items, which they had occupied as chambers, likewise, my body had become a shed. How could I have accommodated such nastiness inside? Things out of use, out of date, and out of order. In that instant, I almost freaked out. Then I made the choice to maintain a composure that would allow a gain. I knew to run away would mean to go insane.

The application of my foresightedness had caused me to do the maths and had left me cringing. If those cockroaches had indeed returned into the shed, chances are, they might breed in larger numbers, in which case, I would have to endure this whole ugly process again. In my mind, I had gone as far as to remember the story of Jesus Christ casting out a demon; that resulted in an undesirable aftermath. It had returned in full force and increased numbers. Thus, I was reminded of the potential of their increase, once more, in a vacant shed. In which case, my fight demanded that I replace a negative item with a positive one.

I put (positive) desire above fear every day.

– Iyanla Vanzant

"Set principles of order" had screamed at me, "The foot spa is meant to be used and not kept in a shed." I was faced with the consequence of an unused item that proceeded to display its existence in a rather ugly manner, in my body, mind, and spirit. A cleansing and clearing had to happen, so that its function could be made available for use. The message was received loud and clear, as I wondered what useful gifts and treasures had been dormant inside of me. That day, I made the choice to trust, like I am trusting now, that I could handle whatever life threw at me, and now, even in the name of set principles of order. From there on, I became mindful, to not only make this a ritual, but to also clear my body and mind frequently, so as to function at my optimum best. Although it could be said that is exactly what life seems to always do: help me to perform at my utmost best.

Evidently, some of the creatures that I encountered had proven strong and huge in overcoming. Even when out, the spot where they had made their homes had been dented, caved in, cracked, and I knew that it was very likely that my internal house, too, needed mending and rebuilding. Although my life at the time was certainly reflective of such disharmony, I could see no obvious signs of ailment or deterioration to my internal house or exactly what needed to be put in order. I could only rely on the idea that my feelings would continue to guide me. And this is the order I now seemed to seek, to remain open to whatever insights are necessary for this journey to the Bridge of Actualising Self-full Love.

Often, as a result of an accident or incident, we are shocked to discover the true state of our health. This led me to conclude that the incident involving Mr. Barack Altidore was an opportunity to heal whatever graze, dents, and cracks needed mending in me. *Like a pruned tree, I will eventually develop new growth with blooming flowers, even brighter than before and with full potential for bearing good fruits. I would be just like the cornfield*, I thought to myself. So once more, I decided to think "a gain"; then, I felt better about the pain. I just kept topping up with the feel good factor, because just as in Christ's teaching of the demon, I knew from experience that the mere overcoming of the sight of some roaches did not mean the end of my process for healing.

Whatever you put your attention on becomes stronger.

Deepak Chopra in his SynchroDestiny program, "Discover the Power of Meaningful Coincidences," asks, "Why are you here?" And I would come up with different answers each time; likewise, I had derived a string of different answers each time I asked myself, Why am I here? My intention of attaining a meaningful resolution had me anticipating a premature yes exclamation. Instead, it seemed like I had been in the land of Wonder for the longest while. All I really knew for sure is that I would know why I was there. I became aware that I had learned at least, to an extent, the importance of set principles of order. Some things just have to be in place before another can be manifested. *What needs to be in place?* I wondered. It was clear that if the answer had not manifested, something else had to be in place, or I must have been blocking it somehow. *So, does this mean I should seek help from Hope for the People? Or is my mind at play again?* I wondered.

Why on earth, under any circumstance, would one make such a choice, to witness a person stepping into the tombed casket, just like that? Again, there are no accidents and no coincidences but the choices that we make. I had repeated this over and over, perhaps as often as had I heard Deepak asking, "Why are you here?" by which I gained myself a mantra.

Then, I heard the soft voice: "You seem alarmed, as though this were your first; have you not witnessed countless incidents such as this before?" If it is that you perceive his act as death, do you not know that many die each day without the actual passing of their last breath, just withering their souls away and without a care in the world? Just remember all humankind's actions lean to either death or life, just flip sides of the same coin. On that note, I concluded that I was not going to be one of those walking dead, no matter what effort it would take to flip in sides.

I had learnt that we often miss the answers we seek because they are so close to us. As often said, we tend to miss what is right underneath our noses. So I decided to pay attention to what was around me. Perhaps that was part of the set principles of order I needed to apply, anyway. "Leave no stone unturned," I reminded myself.

As I deliberately scanned the names of the buildings, I wondered what messages they conveyed. I saw that Final Destination Resort might have meant exactly what it said: a final destination, but was it really, for Mr. Barack Altidore? The thought of permanent relaxation did not appeal to me, even though I felt tired. In fact, it kept me quite awake, as though willing my spirit away from there. Then, there was Hope for the People; a surge of courage immediately ignited my senses, but dwindled as I looked at Grazebrook Primary School. The brook of childhood memories flooded my mind. I was faced with the resurrection of an uncomfortable feeling of attending school without panties on my naked bottom. Obviously, I had been grazed by an incident that seemed impossible to forget. The acronym GPS on the signboard seemed to beckon my attention, as though reminding me that I was in fact operating from my own global positioning system. It felt like a radio station that was requiring me to tune in and was talking to me. As for the pet food warehouse, I could not decipher any possible bearing it might have had at that point, since there was no visible name on it.

In essence, the fact that I still felt affected by my panty-less incident seemed evident of my need for help from HFPT. *I will heal my life and move on with my goal of becoming a movie star, and I will get onto the Bridge of Actualising Self-full Love*, I thought. Even though not everyone recovers from their sickness, I felt that it made sense to consider giving myself the chance of HFTP. My search for meaning had overridden all mundane concerns I may have had. All my senses seemed in readiness for answers, as though each owed all the cells in my body an explanation that would heal them. I proceeded to imagine that it was not just me wanting answers anymore, but thousands of people, even millions, just to ensure that the gods would hear me and would respond accordingly.

"So what did you hear?"

I heard Mr. Altidore asking for the "bloody combination." I also heard the utterance of my own voice asking, "Why did they allow me to sleep in the school?" I had complained that they obviously did not do a Health and Safety Check; otherwise, they would have discovered that I was sleeping in GPS and would awake me before locking up.

What did I smell? A freshness of air, simply hard to define.

What did I taste? A sense of bitter enzyme, like bile wanting to make its way out.

What did I touch? No evidence that I was even there, to see Mr. Altidore stepping into the tombed casket, just like that, since no one had acknowledged my presence anyway. Unless, of course, the dogs could stand in witness for me.

I not only engaged my senses to extremes, but I got the feeling that I was now in search of a treasure box and was hoping it would not be a tombed casket. Strangely, I also got an inkling that like Mr. Altidore, who had Harry to help him unlock the casket, I would have someone to assist me in finding the bloody combination that would unlock my treasure.

The line of continuous internal dialogue had paved tracks in my mind and had formed an unfamiliar highway. So I consoled myself with the neurological reports that claim we have the ability to abandon old thought patterns by creating new pathways in our brains. It sounds rather simple, since all we have to do is be consistently mindful of our new thoughts and behaviours. I felt comfort that perhaps I was onto a good thing.

At that point, I felt I needed a mission statement to endorse my intention. I wanted something that I could anchor onto. Then I would feel prepared for my new mental highway. I would use the words of Emmet Fox from *The Power through Constructive Thinking*. It had been my spiritual wand. Though it is often said, "If it isn't broken, don't fix it." However, I took the view, it's not about waiting till it gets broken to reinforce it. In this case, it just means part of preparing well. Therefore, I would personalise this statement so I could really identify with it, and I would infuse it with fresh, positive thoughts. My magic wand of invisible steel, I will continue to hold it dear, with determination. "Determination" is a word that has worked wonders for me, but if not careful, it can take me to the passing of my last breath. That is why it requires you to be mindful of the degree of force you apply in the use of its ability. Therefore, I now declared, according to Fox's essay, *The Yoga of Love*:

> My mind is made up: I have measured the undertakings; I have counted the cost! It is with "determination" that I intend to joyously attain my desire of getting on to the Bridge of Actualising Self-full Love; thereby reflecting the beauty of the Crimson Light; this intention, or something better, now manifest for me in miraculous satisfying ways; Amen.

This had become my mission statement.

As I continued gazing at the spot of Mr. Altidore's descent, a thought of caution stroked my mind: *Don't be hasty asking questions for the answers that you seek ... for if you become too hasty, you are likely to create numerous options that could result in more confusion.* It would be like getting onto an empty bus, being spoilt for choice, not knowing where to sit. Now even though the explanation made sense, I was unsure why I had not argued and ask why. On the other hand, I might have been appreciating the benefits of tiresomeness, since I had found myself in and out of stillness.

I then became aware, like Mr. Altidore, I had gotten an assistant, but with one exception: Mine was in my head. Now, with the familiar warning voice in my head, I tried to avoid the cut-and-paste solutions of the mind's industrial system of filling in the gap. I wanted to ensure that my experience would invariably make it easy to decipher the truth of what I had seen and why I was there. So, with this firmly in mind, I took the advice of the voice and just stood still there, gazing as though I were recovering from a petit mal seizure.

Simultaneously, after a moment or so, not one but two illusionary entities that I had become acquainted with, for perhaps as long as I have even known myself, Chatterbox and Resignation, were harmoniously in my head, in conversation about Mr. Altidore.

I decided to just observe: a lesson from my spiritual teachers, such as Eckhart Tolle, who often said, "Just observe whatever is going on and remember to make no judgements." He also said to be mindful of yielding to Chatterbox, whose condition is saturated in attention seeking deficit (ASD).

As far as I can recollect, one of my most memorable encounters that I've ever had in my entire life was with that Chatterbox, and it had surely made an impact on me.

I was astounded one day, when I embarked on the name Chatterbox and realised that for a large part of my life, my identity had been encapsulated in Chatterbox. I got to find out, through the Crimson Light, that someone had actually written about me. It happened when I picked up a book from Stoke Newington Bookstore, in North London. Five minutes home, there I was, eagerly going through the pages, when I thought, *Oh my God! I do exist! I recognised myself now; and I'm actually in a book! Wow! Great!*

But somehow, I got the distinct impression that everyone else knew me, excepting myself. How could that have been? But there it was, right before my eyes, in the book *Feel the Fear and Do It Anyway* by Susan Jeffers. *An investment with such profitable returns, though purchased for less than half the normal cost*, I thought to myself.

I also became aware that my ex-boyfriend certainly knew me well because of all the long conversations we had; his longest comment was consistently predictable: "Gur-gur-gurl–you-you- dur-don't don't stop tor-torking you-you- ja-just like -cha-a-a-aChatterbox," and with a big sigh at the end. Honestly, it seemed to me as though "Chatterbox" was the only word he managed to repeatedly utter, each time, in its entirety and without fail for perfect pronunciation. Now, as you can imagine how significant that was for me, since it seemed like I obviously brought out the best in him. I felt good to be called Chatterbox.

My two friends were still carrying on, all this, whilst observing myself, in and out of stillness. Chatterbox buzzing in my head. "One o'clock in the morning, and this is certainly not what I had expected to see; someone stepping in a tomb, just like that?" His intonation suggested I might respond. I did not. Well, not verbally. Even though I was wondering how I had come to find myself there, in time to witness Mr. Altidore's descent. Then I wondered how on earth it took me an hour to step outside the door of GPS? It was not as if I was suffering from some form of agoraphobia or dementia. This was clearly not the case at all. Actually, I had gotten out quite effortlessly.

Why am I here? The thought that I will know everything I need to know, at the right time, space, and sequence, was what I hinged onto with determination. Time, space, and sequence were exactly what I had known, but these factors seemed to cease to exist. As a result, my mission seemed to have changed and consolidated into stillness. In hindsight, I was amazed that I could just observe and not sooner engage with the long-time friend from way past then, Chatterbox.

As though reading out Mr. Altidore's eulogy but with some variation to the norm, Chatterbox began, "Barack Altidore, hmm, Barack Altidore was indeed a fine man of very good character, who was born of St Lucian parents. His mother was English, and his father was French. He had come from a lineage of undertakers. His great-grandfather and grandfather and his father were suppliers of everything to do in the 'transition business.' As an only child, Barack had learnt a lot about how to best handle the dead, including their families." And in a soft whispering kind of tone, Chatterbox said, "I wish we could say the same for whoever is taking care of him down there," and in the same breath, he reverted to his normal tone: "The fact that the man was my friend, I will simply refer to him as Barack, while I continue. Barack was a good man and the best in his profession. He made FDR what it is today. The man was just instrumentally creative. As a cosmetologist and technician, of course, he was responsible for taking care of those in transit. He was the specialist in his field and the best, too! Barack would use aspects of his clients; as though he had the power of bringing them back to life, apart from his own, of course, as though being funny." Chatterbox carried on, "Regardless, whether they went with a smile or their faces long, or looking like the river Nile, the man was simply the best."

Well, he's gone. But how sad that no one can say for sure what drove him to his tomb (or whatever you might call that thing).

Did you know that on top of being the president and owner of this and that (I mean, FDR and being the proprietor of HFTP), Barack was involved in other ventures? Mind you, I can understand why he worked so hard. Let me tell you, some time ago, FDR had made a very big blunder. As a result, it had cost the company a lot of money and even threatened to ruin their reputation. As it happened, it was an extremely busy time for FDR; people were dying like flies. You may not believe this, but the staff ended up accommodating a transitioning visitor into the wrong casket. Well, it was a most startling scene. In the middle of the funeral service, as usual, they uncovered the casket for viewing; that's when they discovered that they had indeed done an incomprehensible blunder. As you can imagine, all the families and friends who had sobbed their hearts out, for hours on end, were just shocked; to say the least. To think of all those tears down their cheeks and smudged make-up for nothing. Not to mention, that was the shortest funeral service I had ever attended.

To resolve the matter, Barack offered the clients a handsome credit voucher of free burials, as buy one, get two free. To see how quickly people are willing to bargain their existence for freeness, the deal was signed and witnessed at the bat of an eyelid. From there on, Barack's effort had helped to restore the reputation of the company, and that was despite the few attendees who attempted to cast a dark shadow on FDR. Of course, with all due caution, they had to go through the whole rigmarole again, and with a nervous congregation, but nevertheless, it turned out to be a successful yet comical event in the end.'

Then again, Barack could sell anybody anything. He was such an eloquent speaker, with a voice that hummed so sweetly that it penetrated the heart strings of almost everyone who heard him. Women were instantly consoled by his melodious voice. Men, on the other hand (excluding me, of course), wished they had a voice such as his, with which they would seduce or console their darlings.'

Then, Chatterbox's voice sounded solemn: "I just don't get it! Forty-seven years; the man was just in his prime. What business did he have stepping into that, whatever you call that thing?" Deadly speaking, Chatterbox then chuckled, as though thinking he was funny, and asked, "Do you think it's anything to do with that GPS case?"

I did not respond, and neither did Resignation, although I admit I was a bit curious about the case. However, being eager to carry on, Chatterbox continued to explain that the parents of the children who attended GPS had won their lawsuit against FDR, but FDR was lucky that they did not have to pay out any money to them. Instead, their only liability was to ensure that their goods would be delivered only at night, and not in the daytime, as was their custom. He said that the aim of the legal action was to combat the large increase of reports of children experiencing nightmares and violent behaviours. That meant many were having trouble concentrating and that inevitably ruined the former high-achieving profile of the Grazebrook Primary School.

Chatterbox continued the eulogy: "The parents felt that the frequent exposure of coffins and body bags, including the constant loading and off-loading of the dead in transit, so close to the school, was definitely the cause of their plight. As part of their legal obligation, FDR was also ordered to make amendments to the front of the building, so as to facilitate customers in and out of the premises with due discretion."

Chatterbox said, "The people of the community of Ti Rocher, Micoud, were becoming particularly concerned in matters of health. That was after the report conducted by urologist Dr. Michael Graven findings that showed that St. Lucians had everything going good for them, apart from the imbalance of sugar intake, which was all they had to 'right.' Basically, they were too sweet! And too much of a good thing, as you know, is as bad as not enough. Now, I am not sure, but it was rumoured that the people thought the selection was a competition. Subsequently, when the researcher reported their findings in 2007, St Lucians was shown to have scored the highest in diabetes and hypertension in the world. As a result, the knock-on effect of their sweetness invariably sky-rocketed the rate of amputees on the island. The number was so high that if they did not make drastic changes to their lifestyle, they would also win the cup the following year. However, when it comes to things like that, St. Lucians just liked to talk; did you hear what they say? Word quickly got around, that the cup for that year was a hoax, and that was when they decided to abandon that position in the human race."

Interesting, I thought, since I have known at least two amputees in my own family. Now according to Chatterbox, that was how St. Lucians changed from amputees to becoming deputies and pioneers in combating concerns of HIV/AIDS through Mother-to-Child Transmission whilst keeping score on general health matters.

"Now you may not have known this," Chatterbox continued, "but Barack had been the forerunner of that movement. In fact, HFTP was inspired from the transformation of St. Lucians.

"I love doing eulogies," Chatterbox said, as though he'd been doing such a fantastic job.

"Now, dead or wherever he's gone, they've discovered that Barack was also the president of that French recycling company in Trinity, Martinique, SadR. That's what I mean; the man was really bright at making things happen! Let me tell you, yes, I think *Seule au de Retour* is what it's called. The company was working on recycling coffins, with the view to broaden their service provision of funeral parlors, in order to meet the individual needs of their prospective customers. It would not only offer people more flexibility but also help them save time and money, which was due to the fact that, for various reasons, people were often unable to attend the funeral of their loved ones. Barack had developed the idea from his experience of business conferences, which he had attended without sharing the physical space with the other attendees. As you know, with technology today, you can sit in your living room or back garden and travel without actually going anywhere. Apart from the option to order a one-way or two-way casket, that's what Seule au de Retour was about.

"The idea SadR was hoping to propose was relatively simple." It sounded as though Chatterbox was trying to sell this idea. "It was designed so that you could attend a funeral service virtually anywhere in the world whilst simultaneously experiencing the actual event as it is happening and making your presence felt. However, the main challenge was that St. Lucians on the whole just love to socialise in their traditional way and especially hate the idea of missing out on the Last Supper, so to speak (even though the one in whose honour it is being presented has ceased to exist). Can you imagine changing traditions of burying the dead? Traditions that have been there since BC?"

"Barack was a workaholic, dealing with so many dead people, day in day out, and night in night out, too! You know what I mean?"

I was thinking, *Chatterbox is definitely an information collector, you know, like those on the* Antique Road Show. You've seen them on TV, of course? He was just moving from one item to the next.

Despite all that, I began to think about the custom that takes place, at the passing of loved ones on the island. I could not help but wonder how SadR's idea would apply for the wake, where the locals in the community come together to comfort the bereaved. Then, as the urge came to voice my opinion, Resignation, in his low voice, said, "Just be objective! For the power of the Crimson Light can shine on anything and anyone, and at any time."

Immediately, I knew what Resignation meant: I should just listen without the need to influence others, because there are no accidents and no coincidences, only the choices that we make.

"Well," Chatterbox continued, "after his wife had died, and since both his daughters were grown, he ended up developing quite a reputation with the ladies. Who knows? Perhaps it had something to do with the flowers. Let me tell you, I knew another undertaker named Troy. He was a piece of work, that one. You'd never guess what he did. Troy tricked his wife for several years; practically every day, he brought her lovely, fresh flowers. That was, until she found the little card inside that read, 'In Loving Memory of My Dear Mother.' Consequently, it all boomeranged right in his face, losing his whole family."

I thought, 'what a sad story and yet amusing whilst I struggled to maintain my state of composure as I listened to Chatterbox.

Just when I thought he'd finish talking, sounding even more off track than before, and in a louder pitch, Chatterbox exclaimed, "I think it was his lifestyle, burning the candle at both ends: that would be enough to drive anyone to their grave; in Barack's case … whatever you call that thing."

But in all seriousness, he continued, "Deadly speaking, here's what I think. I think the pressure of his deadly career drove him mad."

Chatterbox, with his "deadly" spree in my ears, though most annoying, was certainly getting my attention, especially when he mentioned pressure, because a lot of people die of pressure. My mother died of high blood pressure, and for a while, I had found myself on the borderline. Plus, it has been reported to be the main cause of various illnesses, including strokes.

Psychologists claim that you can hold only one thought at a time. It felt as though I was holding everything that Chatterbox had said, but in one huge capsule that took the size of my mouth, with the instructions, "Only to be taken once a lifetime, or run the risk of a fatal attack, if exceeded."

After a while, it felt like I had been attending church service and had passed lunch time. Your stomach grumbles, yet the preacher still carries on, while you anticipate the end of his closing words. A series of sarcastic "Amens" are echoed across the congregation, because "Amen" is all one can say then. Nothing personal, but that's because everyone's hungry; yet, does he get it? Absolutely not! However, with Resignation, I still exclaimed "Amen" to Chatterbox's speech, and that was perhaps just to comfort myself that I did something.

Resignation has always been the quieter of my two friends. He is the type you can reply on, "Whatever you say …" For me, that is a good thing, but sometimes, when needing a little guidance or encouragement, "Whatever you say" is not what I want to hear. However, he always makes his presence felt, often in the subtlest of ways; even then, I know he means well. There were times, though, I felt that Resignation was responsible for a lot of traumas in my life. I wanted to see him standing up for me. I wanted to hear him say, "Oh, no, not on my watch," or something to that effect. Resignation and I had lots of arguments about that. Well, I would do most of the talking whilst he listened. God, it took me a long time to understand and learn how to accept Resignation, in good spirit. One thing I can tell you for sure: Whenever I experienced a transformation of any kind, Resignation was always involved. For this reason, I would often remind myself of his loyalty, even though he never seemed to remain throughout the process.

"Deadly speaking, let's face it: Barack's line of business was not an easy one; especially having to deal with all sorts of difficult people. Dealing with the dead is the easy part. But when it comes to friends and families of the dearly and merely departed, that's when you get to see people in their true colours. You know what I mean?" Chatterbox kept blabbering on.

"For instance, I know of a case where some families and friends were so enmeshed in suitcases of perceived necessities of their departed. Some were picking and choosing items as though preparing for their annual vacations, whilst others were grieving over goodbyes that they did not get a chance to say. There were others too; wrestling with frictions that'd remained unsettled, including their last words of hate uttered, without even the slighted chance of resolution. Can you imagine?

"On top of that, you'll find family and friends always blaming someone else for their departed in transit. If it's not someone's fault, then it's an institution like Hope for the People. To them, the care should be enough to keep their loved ones going on forever and a day."

Apart from raising my concerns about coming out alive from HFTP, while I considered what he had said to be true, Chatterbox had failed to mention the question of unnatural death that is prevalent on the island. Often, it requires at least one person who didn't like the deceased enough to call him a *Maji Nwe* (if male) or a *Maji Blan* (if female) as a practitioner of evil. Thus, always someone claiming to have executed the death just to seem unbeatable at the game.

Resignation and I were still subjected to the constant chatter of our friend as he continued, "Now there are those who resent others for taking charge in handling the affairs, and all the palaver that entails the rituals of final goodbyes. Often claiming to have more rights than others, like who is going to keep the wedding band and other sentimental objects, whilst no one admits the truth that the majority of them are wondering about the will and who is going to get what? God forbid that someone feels entitled to something but is left out of the will. What happens then, in cases of no will? Often, people fight, or a secret loved child shows up to make his claim, or to simply be recognised. Everyone's world tends to turn upside down. Enough said, may my dear friend Barack Altidore rest in peace."

I couldn't agree more. As though unlocking my brain, Chatterbox had pulled the lid of my experiences and highlighted the fact that we were engaged in fighting over material stuff.

It could be said that the formality of preparing a will, for example, demonstrates one's intentions for peace as she sees fit, but also an acknowledgement that she will eventuality be faced with the passing of her last breath. Even though only subjective, but that in itself becomes reflective of the quality of the relationships she held with people, things, and events. In this case, final testaments are drawn with cruel, as well as good, intentions. This leads me to take the view that perhaps for many, the focus of a will as a final testimony does not in itself serve the totality of preparing well at all, that is, since the final will and testimony can cause as much friction as the absence of one. In such cases, the legacies that are meant to serve as benchmarks for others strips families apart and results in disharmony, whereby we increasingly lose all sense of self. *Nevertheless,* I thought, *Chatterbox certainly has his use.*

I became curious to uncovering the determining factors that often rippled out, as if a stone had been thrown into a muddy pond. For instance, if you are embarking on the journey of actualising self-full love, you may not be too perturbed about niceties and wedding bands and other sentiments. However, the practicality and set principles of order seem to definitely have its place in our race, and that's why, according the proverbial verse, "A man should see well to his business," which invariably brings the question to mind: Can one be concerned about life without being concerned about death; or growth without stagnation; or love without hate? Or even forgiveness without concerns of grievance; or peace without concerns of haste? To me, it would seem crucial that I am not only able to differentiate the polarities that affect me but understand how I can best use them for my quest in attaining the highest good life offers. Would that not mean to consider my relationship under the umbrella of life and death?

Set principles of order was screaming at me once more and had beckoned the questions: Would I be willing to let go? Would I be willing to hold on? For these are the choices I must make, so that peace would reign even when I cease to exist. Would I be willing to allow myself to be the sacred ground, like the cornfield? If so, then I certainly have to be healed. So far, everything was pointing to the quality of relationships I would need to cultivate.

Although I am thankful to no longer be referred to as Chatterbox, I maintained my gratitude, for it is said, "In all things, give thanks." I felt truly grateful for the opportunity that had proven my competence to listen without interference and an appreciation that I had gained a clearer picture of who Mr. Altidore was. I became excited about how the dance of polarities might play out in my life. The emergence of butterflies and optimism synthesised in my stomach and made evident that my desire of the Crimson Light was operating in me. Then, as I wondered what it might seem like to be on the Bridge of Actualising Self-full Love, I felt a glow had enveloped me once more. I knew I would always be safe.

Anchoring Points

There are no accidents and no coincidences, but the choices we
make: Today, I am making a choice to see from different
realms,
perspectives, and
senses.

I am now open and receptive to the guidance of the Crimson
Light; therefore, I am trusting the choice I have made to
look,
question, and
assimilate.

For true peace of mind, we must acknowledge
Whatever fault we live upon,
Whatever time bomb ticks in our closet,
And enjoy our Shangri-la nonetheless.
It isn't the absence of the problem:
It is how one lives in its presence that matters.
– Chungliang Al Huang

Chapter Three

The Crimson Light
through the Darkness

Step by step, I decided to explore the events that had caused me to wonder, Why am I here? There certainly was no obvious need for the bunch of silver keys that had showed up in the palm of my right hand. I mean, it's not as though I needed them to make my exit from GPS, neither were they necessary for observing Mr. Barack Altidore, stepping into the tombed casket, just like that. Having consolidated a flood of ideas, I felt that perhaps they are meant to help me unlock the mysteries that now concerned me.

Despite the gloomy nature of Mr. Altidore's descent, I still found a degree of comfort in exploring both sides of the coin, like life and death. That gave me confidence to believe that where there are questions, so too, there must be answers. Therefore, I accepted the responsibility that I must have consented to whatever was blocking the answers I was seeking. It became evident that I was faced with what appeared as an unknown cause for my condition. My soul felt in need of healing. A beam of light seemed to pivot my attention on the pool of information I had seen and heard. Unwavering thoughts of Mother's death had captured my mind, or was it the realisation that I had been held ransom for the question that had never really left me?

But why? I wondered: *Why do we do what we do?*

Normally after a tragic event, you are likely to hear, "Oh well, what can you do? Life goes on" or "You got to get on with life," thus giving the impression it's time to move on. It also emphasises the point that if you cannot do anything to change a situation or event, the quicker you accept that reality, the better it would be for you (and all others concerned). That stance, however, also implies that one should not dwell on the past. In trying to determine what that means, in itself, often renders little encouragement to explore the cause and initial impact of the loss one might be experiencing. To examine the cause, also, compels one to look and to really focus on the situation at hand, whilst running the risk of feeling worse than before. Therefore, it's easy to see why one would rather yield to the temptation to avoid exploring his pain. That was the stance I took when Mother died in August 1993. Evidently, my mind had become saturated with statements that made getting on with life seem easy.

As painful as our experiences were of Mother's passing, it seemed like my siblings got on with life, as well, so I could not risk being left behind; even though I cannot claim to know what is in the heart of another. The initial impact of my loss of Mother appeared to have weaned off fairly quickly. I suppose it was so because I had taken on the view that her spirit would always be with me. Subsequently, whenever I had done something that I thought was typical of her, I would acknowledge it as her presence being with me, and this invariably would affirm my belief. This happened to be one of the quickest arithmetical solutions I had solved. The urgency of the matter had become a fight-or-flight response for self-preservation. To have considered otherwise felt as though I would lose my head. According to the proverbial wisdom, "Why cut your nose to spite your face?" After all, I was no longer experiencing grief of my loss; well, not consciously anyway. The Crimson Light was so gentle with me and had yielded me a sort of peace.

On one hand, getting on with life embodies a number of facets that require our attention. While we may appear to be stagnant in certain areas, we actually move towards other zones. In reality, this does not necessarily mean that we have moved on in terms of our loss or disappointment, simply because our attention has been diverted elsewhere. In many cases, such items are left to simmer like pots on the back burners, waiting to be attended. Everyone knows what happens to unattended items in such cases.

Now, I learned that all emotional experiences are derivative of either fear or love. Therefore, it is on this basis I concluded that perhaps I had been in denial of the impact of Mother's passing, for the fear of experiencing too great a loss. If that were true, then this would ultimately mean that I was in grave danger of putting too many items on the back burner, so to speak. I felt that, to not attend to my sense of loss would be to risk having to face an unrecognisable item and, most definitely, one without substance.

For instance, I once found myself crying uncontrollably over what I thought was a meaningless matter that involved my then boyfriend. Afterwards, on exploring the possible cause of my wallow, which had left me totally exhausted, I discovered that it was really about my feeling of losing Mother. And I had even found myself in the same physical space that I had occupied at the time of hearing the news of her passing. My dispositions and sensations at the time led me to confront what had been simmering in my gut and had surfaced so unexpectedly. In essence, the argument had only served as a key for unlocking the door by which the imprisoned emotion escaped. How would it be, if I could not have concisely tagged that emotion at all, simply because it had become distorted? That observation showed, unless I wanted to risk the label of being mentally unstable with the inability to validate my behaviour, I would need to address my issues and hopefully unblock the right answers into existence.

Nearly each variable Chatterbox had spoken, regarding Mr. Altidore's eulogy, had its threads stitched and knotted in the makeup of our family fabric. Mother's passing was our first significant family loss. That reality had invariably begat itself in each yarn, as it did in each child. Perhaps, for this reason, though not consciously, we endeavoured to salvage the tapestry of life that we felt had kept us as a unit. Suddenly, all that it had represented was exposed. Like blood cells rushing to protect a gushing wound, so it was for us as we bravely did what was both naturally and culturally required of us. In turn, I got the impression that it was also meant as sufficient for our healing and to get on with life.

It is true what Chatterbox said, that death resurrects a lot to the surface, but in hindsight, death still beckons us to life. Because even then, I felt that the Crimson Light had breached through our sadness, whilst protruding fleeting rays as though they'd derive from behind the spaces of high-rise buildings, and yet ensuring to allow the feel of dancing tree branches of the dense forest: the dark feeling of Mother's passing. It was that dance through the darkness that kept us together; we were able to lean on each other. I suppose it was because we felt each other's pain, as though a covert consensus had taken place between us, so we knew exactly what to convey, ensuring each one was provided a portion of love.

The love we shed had reflected our capacity to exercise good manners and have respect for our elders, which had been instilled in us, as strong family values. I had over time considered our religious teaching and practices as just illusions of sacred togetherness; I had not permitted myself to appreciate the benefits until then. In hindsight, the splendour of the Crimson Light, through the darkness and the pain of death, had also rendered us bliss; thus, bringing the words to life: "Where there is one, so you shall find the other," just flip sides of the same coin.

Did the light shine for us because we had consented to it, by just acknowledging our pain and sense of loss? Like I had wondered, did the light shine for me because I had consented to be a witness to Mr. Altidore's descent? I felt such questions might help to establish the patterns that had, up until now, mapped out my life; especially if I was that sick, to want to witness Mr. Altidore's presumed suicide. So I also questioned what conditions I was to acknowledge and that I would consent to the healing of my wounds. In which case, I would not find myself just breaking down anywhere or risk feeling the need to step into a tomb.

I remembered crying out for help on hearing the news of Mother passing, "Dear God, I need your help! Please, make me to be strong like Mother was." There, I had given my consent, immediately.

On reflection, I discovered that the Crimson Light consists of everything good and pure, because I could always pray to be on the other side of life that I didn't like. However, the illumination of the Crimson Light working through the darkness taught me a vital lesson, that not everything I dislike is necessarily bad or unhealthy for me: a lesson I am still undergoing in the Open University of Life. Like, even reminiscing over Mother's passing, which I sense might be good for me.

Although I had not concluded whether my feelings were of denial or guilt, for thinking that I had gotten on with life, but I was faced with the "ransom" of confusion that felt like a gun to my head. Like deliberately avoiding the core of an apple, I nibbled around the subject of Mother passing. This, in turn, helped me to affirm with determination, leaving no stone unturned.

Getting on with life and with its strain on our family fabric had, consequently, caused a few rips here and there. As time went by, it seemed as though the glue of empathy, love, and compassion for each other had expired and gone dry. Instead, there was the feeling that each mind had become overshadowed by various life conditions that played the game of hide and seek, and left some of us in perpetual isolation, still waiting to be found.

Oh, how I often wished those shadows would change their position
And be forgotten into the sleep of the night;
Besides, the morning dew would gleam with brightness,
Where no one needs seek that, which is not hidden.

Developing healthy relationships can prove challenging with life's ups and downs, and that requires time, trust, and being vulnerable in order to overcome. It would have seemed that the cohesion I continued to crave was partly because of this lack. Even though our lives on many occasions revealed the general state of affairs of many families on the island, with siblings living in various households of extended family and friends. Not to mention the fact that many would also travel abroad, in search for a better life.

The sad occasion of Mother's passing had drawn together eight brothers and four sisters, from England, America, Canada, the Virgin Islands, and elsewhere. In addition, there were also other siblings of Mother's husband, with the exception of two brothers, who were unable to travel at the time.

In retrospect, I had not considered to what extent we might have been affected, not only through the loss of Mother but also in terms of our relationships with each other. The younger ones of course knew me from photographs and visits to the island. Overall, there was an absence of frequent and direct communication. For instance, being just two years ahead of me, my sister Sylvia and I bonded, but it was not until my early teens. We had walked miles to the farm, where we picked pigeon peas. Sylvia had developed a strategy of how we could work very quickly, with an urgency to impress our parents with our harvest. She had suggested that we work on opposite sides of the row, picking peas and dropping them into heaps, which we later bagged up. She was a very bright, quiet, but confident individual, which meant she was loved and admired by everyone who knew her. Not only that, she was the perfect school prefect, but she was also the perfect youth prefect in church. Sylvia was the kind of girl every mother, including mine, wanted their daughters to be like. Mother said to me, "Why can't you be like her?" Perhaps for the fact that Sylvia had a range of talents and loved to wear long-length clothes, which made her more appealing to the decent eye.

We had continued the momentum of chatting and laughing, from home, as we teased each other through the spaces between the branches that also provided us shade from the beaming sun. The fun was hyped more, especially when she got a little caterpillar, or pretended to have gotten one, by flashing a light branch in my face (because I was petrified of caterpillars). Nevertheless, we giggled a lot that day.

Suddenly, we came to a halt. Something had gotten into my right eye. Sylvia was still laughing while I desperately tried to alert her that my complaint was very serious, so as to get her attention to remove whatever was there. The antidote that we both knew was to blow as hard as possible into the troubled eye, so that whatever it was would fly right out. Silvia blew several times, which seemed more like spitting into my eye, and on the application of each dose, she would let go of my eyelids, so that I could check if the thing was still there, or gone.

"Still there!" I said, after the fifth time or so; she suddenly burst into a hilarious bout of laughter, followed by several attempts to blow simultaneously. "What are you laughing at?" I asked, and then I asked again, several times before she could contain herself: "Why are you laughing?"

Trying to catch her breath, she replied, "If you could see what I see, I'm telling you, and if you weren't my sister, I would leave you right there!" She was still laughing.

"Why?" I said.

"Girl, if you could see the size of your eyeball, that is so big!"

At that stage, we were both in stitches, laughing about how I'd frightened her. You can imagine, we could not stop, and this continued at each subsequent attempt to blow air stroke spit into my eye. Yes, that day I discovered that, apart from the long list of scientifically proven benefits of laughter, it is also a good antidote for a troubled eye. Since that day we couldn't stand a "spitting" chance for saving my eye.

As the taste of that reminiscence filled my mind once more, I felt perhaps I needed laughter. I then gave myself permission to laugh on reflection of the sick joke about the undertaker that gave his wife flowers that belonged to the dead. In so doing, I began sensing the dance of heads and tails; eventually, I would be able to wrap my head around what really mattered.

Although not much else to laugh about, but it seemed sufficient to continue my endeavour, I thought.

Most of us, including Silvia, Richard, Bruno, and I, lived with Auntie Lyle, since her only child, lived abroad, and grandmother, who happens to be both Auntie Lyle's and Mother's mother. We were what psychology would today regard as a dysfunctional family. Yet I have also experienced and witnessed strong positive bonds amongst us. That meant, some things worked well. For instance, we have always known how to laugh. We knew how to laugh at ourselves and others, of course. Particularly in the days of no television, we entertained each other. Pitching marbles, skipping around, and playing various ball games, which always bore the risk of getting severely hurt, was not to be missed. For instance, you would not want to get hit by the homemade melted-down nylon ball used for playing cricket, which could cause permanent damage. But if you did, you could still expect to get laughed at, on top of your plight. Typically, if anyone of us had got beaten by our parents (which was often by our father, Mr. All-Bags Full), there would always be at least one witness to laugh at you. If it were not by a sibling, at least there would be a neighbour or two, trying to add salt to the wound: "Oh yes! You got a good beating!" As though it had occurred in the absence of your awareness. Yet it leaves you thinking, *Tell me something I don't know.*

I don't recall ever finding the humour in such cases. For that reason, I took great offense when I was mocked. They found it funny the way I jumped and skipped from the beating of Mother's husband, Mr. All-Bags-Full. The scenario would be me, trying to get away from him as quick as possible so that I could get to the tamarind tree. Though a few yards away, it never seemed close enough for my rescue. You see, if I made it in time, I would not have to endure, on top of all else, the embarrassment of indecently peeing down my legs.

The beatings, however, were not the only indignation I had to endure from Mr. All-Bags-Full. Religiously, as part of my day job, I had to dispose the contents of his pail into the outhouse, which was no more than three to four meters away from the home. I didn't understand why on earth I was designated to dealing with such a shitty job. Imagine going to bed, knowing that the first thing you had to face in the morning is the stench of a big man's poop. It's not as though he was disabled. Furthermore, I don't recall ever signing up for that, and neither do I recall seeing any of my siblings dealing with what I had to do. With no formal shadowing, I just had to deal with this thing on my own.

Since I felt somewhat like Cinderella, with no hope of freedom that I could be rescued by a handsome prince, I decided to take the matter into my hands. Well, at least to deal with it another way. Although I had previously failed in several attempts to win one over Mr. All-Bags-Full, I was still determined that I'd win one day. Each attempt was increasingly showing me what I might have had to face. I did the brave thing, one day, and left the damn poop baking in the hot sun. I knew I ran the risk of being punished and thought that I might have to face one of the most unpleasant sights of all, but I was determined. I still did it. In hindsight, I think it was then that I adopted Determination as one of my favourite allies.

As it turned out, it was one of the longest days of my life, since my mind was so occupied with thoughts of a possible nightmare that my action (or inaction) would boomerang right in my face. The time had come to put an end to the mental torture I had endured the whole day. Mother and Mr. All-Bags-Full had returned home. In a matter of minutes, Mother asked me why I had left the "treasure pail" unattended. Before I could respond, Mr. All-Bags-Full butted in, "See, your queen sits in the house all day; so lazy and nasty, and she doh even empty dee pail!" After asking a second time, with my heart beating like a drum, I said, "Mom, I am tired! I am really tired of doing that."

Mother told me, "I understand, but just do it for the last time. I will make sure you won't have to do it again."

Mother told him off, and he was obviously very unhappy.

Having done the maths, I knew I couldn't just throw away the pail. The impact of the hot sun had literally given rise to the matter. Consequently, the process proved longer and more tedious than I could imagine, especially for the fact that the consistency had left a tough circle inside. Even after it had been soaked, I was actually faced with the matter in my bare hands, literally. It was a race trying to complete the task against the duration of holding my breath, and just to avoid taking in the stench, I had to ensure that I kept my mouth shut, literally. Afterwards, I concluded, perhaps that's the way battles are won; they get far worse before they get better. In spite of the nasty victory that night, I went to bed feeling that I had actually found a real treasure: a moment of simple bliss. I had learnt one of life's serious lessons: that in order to gain your victories, you must be willing to pay the cost.

Mr. All-Bags-Full was a very handsome man and was perceived as a well-to-do individual in the community. He was a successful farmer, apart from his many other gifts and talents; an entrepreneur in his time, and certainly, in his own rights, a road maker, cock fighter, professional gambler, and the seed-sewer of about eighteen children.

Mr. All-Bags-Full knew how to win friends and influence people. Though illiterate, he had friends and acquaintances from all walks of life, from the fisherman to the prime minister. He was equipped with a wide range of social skills, including the common language of persuasion, such as "You scratch my back and I'll scratch yours" or "Exchange is no robbery." In addition was the language of money that never fails to influence others. As a farmer, Mr. All-Bags-Full took great pride in his produce. He had a knack for balancing various projects simultaneously with success rates. Somehow, he managed to handle his affairs admirably well. Although we did not get on well, in my heart, I was hypocritically proud to be associated with him, because, while he was influential, it tore me inside to see Mother struggle to provide us our basic needs.

I was privileged to have witnessed the joy he expressed after he had proudly learnt how to write his four-letter name. I mean his Christian name, and with accuracy too. Though the family joke was that one day, Mr. All-Bags-Full had presented his name with the last letter missing, and Mother asked why it was so; he directed her to the bar on which the pen had run, having passed the edge of the paper. He said, "Go and see for yourself, if you don't believe me." He was funny like that. Being able to write his name was quite an achievement.

He was called Mr. All-Bags-Full because, as a worker on his farm, you would not make a trip with your bag half-full; that is, if he thought you could carry a bigger load than you did. With him around, you were expected to stretch beyond your ideals. There were standards that as an employee, you knew you had to adhere to. For example, everyone knew that if they fell down with a load on their head, which was a common possibility, particularly when it rained;

they would have to answer to him. Sometimes, workers covered for one another to avoid being reprimanded. Digging your toes in the muddy pathways was never a guarantee to stop you slipping or falling down with your load. Climbing up and going down hills demanded the skills of balance and good reflexes on the paths of sticks and stones, including other sharp objects, like pieces of glass and prickles. Furthermore, depending on the circumstance of you tripping to the ground, his view could consequently denote a negative of the object of your attention.

You had to report your case just as in today's modern time of filling in incident/accident reports: What time did the incident occur? Who was present when the incident happened? This would follow a host of other questions of exacerbation, with the exception of, What safety measures could you have taken to minimise the risk of this happening in the future? In lame terms, "Was the banana bruised? If so, how many fingers were bruised? How much were you able to save?" And he would end his speech: "By the way doh let it happen again; otherwise, you're fired!"

I suppose, the way Mr. All-Bags-Full saw it, people can heal their bruises and get over their pain, because then everyone was responsible for his own injuries. But the produce in which he had invested time, money, and labour proved a significant loss when damaged. It was his way of letting us know to be mindful of our actions. Often, not to cause friction, I would fill the bag; apart from when it came to carrying bananas, which would be one or two bunches, the most at a time, depending on size. Other crops would include breadfruits, corn, coconuts, dasheens and yams, pumpkins, sweet potatoes, and watermelon. The melons were so big and heavy that often, I could only handle one at a time. We had to be extra careful, because if one falls to the ground that would be it – busted or smashed! However, busted or smashed would not mean wasted. It would justify the means to feast upon the nourishing foods that had been carefully selected for the market.

A twisted pad would be made for your head, with dry banana leaves, with the chance of being bitten by a tarantula or by those little red ants, for that matter.

Now my last batch on the farm was carrying ginger. I knew for a fact that I worked hard then and had made my name as a good worker, even with Mr. All-Bags-Full. I didn't need anyone telling me how much to carry, because by then, I had become a professional at the game. I had even heard him telling Mother how hard I worked that season. This was probably one of the nicest things I had heard him say about me; that was, apart from sarcastically referring to me as Mother's "*la Reine*," which means "queen" in Creole, the other language alongside English spoken on the island. Had it been known to me at the time, I might have been tempted to relish the idea that I was indeed royal and would attempt to make an impressionable appearance as being queen. As it happened, I did not need his validation, but at the time, it made me feel good that I actually did something that pleased him. In retrospect, that's exactly the reason I worked so hard.

It was me and Shabine (a very skinny, light-skinned female); the two of us, we had dealt with that ginger good and proper. Shabine had gained her PhD in the field with flying colours and had become my mentor. Up to this day, I still wonder how she managed to carry such a big load with a waistline that seemed to measure only about eighteen inches.

It would have to be the enjoyable aroma of the ginger impacting on my nervous system that kept me going. I gained the courage and strength to have my bags full, bearing in mind we would have fewer trips to endure in the baking sun. Shabine and I were trusted to do our work without interference of having someone looking over our shoulders. I finally had something to feel really good about; I had proven my competence in the hard labour market. The allegiance of the Crimson Light had enabled me to enjoy a degree of confidence in myself, despite the darkness I hid so deep inside.

Though unawares at the time, I realised it had been my faithful friend Resignation who had nudged me onto my side and reminded me, I was no longer an undergraduate on the farm. You see, like the bunch of keys that had showed up in the palm of my hand, I was ready to use my degree to unlock the doors of a new life. The Crimson Light was beckoning me into a different direction, one in which *I could wear fine clothes and high heels; I won't have much to do with dirt anymore,* I told myself. The time came to put on the grand finale in preparation for my exit, not only from the farm but also from home. After a long process of approximately two years, I would finally go to England, the long-dreamt place of my birth. There I would meet my biological father and my sisters. *Perhaps things will be better with that family,* I often thought. The Crimson Light would brighten my path through the dark tunnel, and I would see the light.

Anchoring Points

There are no accidents and no coincidences, but the choices
we make: Today, I am making a choice to handle
pain,
hope, and
uncertainty.

I am now open and receptive to the guidance of the Crimson
Light; therefore, I am trusting the choice I have made to be
daring,
insightful, and
enquiring.

The Imprisoned Splendour

Truth is within ourselves; it takes no rise from outward things,
what e'er you may believe.
There is an inmost centre in us all,
Where truth abides in fullness; and around, wall upon wall,
the gross flesh hems it in,
This perfect clear perception which is truth.
A baffling and perverted carnal mesh binds it, and makes all error;
and to know rather consist in opening out a way.
Whence the imprisoned Splendour may escape,
than in effecting entry for a light supposed to be without.
– Robert Browning

CHAPTER FOUR

The Ties that Bind

It was like trying to remember why you entered into a room, because you'd forgotten what you went in for in the first place, so I had to backtrack in exploring the mystery around my seeing Mr. Barack Altidore stepping into the tomb casket, just like that.

I had woken in the school lounge at exactly midnight. I was certain that the time on the wall had showed eleven o'clock sharp, just before shutting my eyes to sleep on the red sofa, which seemed like the only trendy piece of furniture in the entire building. I had not intended to sleep for a long period of time, but neither did I give thought to waking up at a specific time, as I normally would do.

I felt like a force had moved me to a specific door, which was the only form of exit. The door, which went through a six-inch-thick wall, was firmly erected on the left side, thus forming a wedged angle that allowed a gap with just sufficient space to go through at a right angle. Still, with no obvious need for the keys in my hand, I made my exit, to the warm reception of two guard dogs looking directly into my eyes, followed by an unexpected and inexplicable brightness outside.

How could this be? I thought. Yet I had entered the first hour of a new day. I knew that it could not have taken more than a minute to step through the door. Please don't ask me how I knew the time;

once outside, I just knew. And that was just before seeing Mr. Barack Altidore step into the tombed casket, just like that.

His descent gave me a sense of stillness, yet with much inner dialogue: stillness that assured me of peace and that all I needed was right there and that was a safe place to be, inner dialogue that seemed to convey a process necessary for self-acceptance that I had made the choice to be there. Now, it was no longer the soft, gentle voice that I heard before, and certainly not Chatterbox or Resignation, but rather a knowing.

I was replaying Mr. Altidore's motion in my head, and I had not stopped wondering about the jumpin time. It was as though I had three separate selves all doing their own thing, simultaneously, all at the same time. Yet time had ceased to exist and was only significant in terms of the fact I still felt a sense of misery, and that despite his eulogy, I felt there was more. It was the resurrection of all kinds of stuff that concerned me, mainly pertaining to my issues around Mother's funeral. My thoughts were being played by my three separate selves, as if picking up the same pieces of a puzzle, trying to make them fit. Still, the picture that I needed to understand was incomplete.

My mind was quickly flooded with the same questions as before, including the lump in my throat that felt as if it had a name. "Where do I stand now? Will I remain a secret even to my siblings, those who were not aware that I have a different father from them? But they call me sis, anyway; do they even know or simply call me sis, (meaning sister)?"

I wanted to know, because there is a difference if someone just likes and appreciates you for who you are and have a sense of biological obligation, because they think that is what is expected of them. I wasn't even sure whether I had the right to address this issue. Did I possess the skill to address the matter? Again, I felt overpowered with guilt. It seemed too soon. After all, even though a week had passed by, she was not yet laid in the ground.

The locals in the community of the family home, too, had their host of questions about me, for some knew the truth, and some didn't. The occasion was perfect for the information collectors, to gratify their curiosity.

As I passed by, I could hear them saying, "Who is this one?"

"Oh, she's the one who lives in London?"

"Yes, but did you know, that one is not the husband's …?"

"Really?"

Others had indicated a need to hear it straight from the horse's mouth, so to speak; I gladly confirmed their findings. "How is Lorraine? She's your sister, isn't she?" She was my ffriend. That was a sure way of connecting the dots between the two families.

Speaking of my siblings, by either parent of my two families was often an arkward subject. Particularly when referring to those not of the immediate households but commonly referred to as "those outside"; I prefer to call them "fringes." At least a Fringe is expected to have character and represent a demarcation. Maybe, it's because of the 'outside' terminology, 'fringes' (in my opinion) tend to look more like their fathers than the 'insider' so to speak. This perhaps is to ensure their idendity. My arkwardness was often about the need to explain the position of another sibling which in turn would reflects my own position as a fringe, and that invariably would present a line of questioning that I had not initially anticipated.

"Did you say your father passed away here in London?"

"I thought both your parents lived in St Lucia."

"Oh, I had a different father than my other siblings."

"So I take it, you are your mother's first child?"

"No!"

Often before I would conclude my answer, they would say, "Oh, you must be the last, then?"

"No, I am the fifth child of my mother's, and the last child of my father's."

"I suppose your mother was unmarried when she had you."

"No, she was married."

The feeling of intrusion would foster a need to conceal what I felt inside, even in my directness to seem real. I would hide my mother's infidelity, which I felt represented an ugly truth. The truth that I felt, my mother had been judged, had indeed caused me to hide. A truth that had formed the yardstick of being judged by the opposite sex, who perceived me as a classic subject for infidelity. I would hide myself from myself. That truth became my preoccupation to layer my mind with thoughts that cement my fears of any cracks, so that I would not forget to continue to hide.

Yet, still I grieve?

Could it be the severe beating that I had gotten, to never again repeat, "Mr. All-Bags-Full is not my real father"? Did I fail in that quest, even as an adult, to conceal the secret, but deep down, I wanted it known that "I am different yet of the same tapestry."

No doubt that Mother was the emblem of that tapestry, and she was the good one. How could she die before him? *Is it not true, that long life is meant to be a blessing?* I asked myself. Then I remembered those who came into this world and transited, just hours of being on this plane, some just minutes, so I consoled myself, but yet with another truth that I had not understood altogether.

Why did it have to be that way?

Mother had always tried her best to "save the children," excluding me, from the severe beatings of Mr. All-Bags-Full. After her earlier attempts had failed, she refrained from being accused of bias towards me. Otherwise, I would be punished more severely than initially intended. When it came to being punished by Mr. All-Bags-Full, you would have to be lucky to get away. Perhaps with Mother's persuasion, you could escape from the numbers of lashes and the severity of the brown leather belt often worn around his waist. It always seemed like a whole ritual would be taking place, before getting started. I think it was his way of warming up. After removing the belt, Mr. All-Bags-Full would tie a knot with both ends at the waist of his pants, to stop them from dropping to the ground. In retrospect, it was a funny sight, but back then, it did not allow the indulgence of laughter, particularly if you were the one getting thrashed with the belt. No doubt your attention would be to minimise the impact of each lash, by trying to get away.

Other instruments used for punishments involved tree branches, often with the leaves peeled off, a specification Mr. All-Bags-Full often demanded of me. It was so, as to make a profound impact on contact against my body. Leafless whips and a piece of rubber hose was sealed in my name. I learnt very quickly not to waste time by bringing a small whip, so I would not have to endure a long process by changing the size. My attitude was to get it over and done with, instead of going into hiding, like some of my brothers often did; they would still end up getting beaten.

Somehow, I could always tell that Mother was not happy when he would beat me, but she rarely verbalised her disapproval. Furthermore, I had seen her get slapped by him a few times, too. I always felt that my beatings were unjustified and were more frequent and severe than my siblings. Explaining my case was never going to be a saving grace. After a while, I just resolved to endure the pain without trying to talk myself out of it. Yet I was always presented the question, what happened? I think it was for the purpose to validate his actions.

My resilience had become like tar and, perhaps, just as black as Mr. Altidore's smoky hole. On one occasion, the end of the strap had imprinted on my face, and the skin had even peeled off. About two days later, on my return to school, the teacher, Mrs. Promise, asked, "What happened *to you*?" The words "to you" meant something to me; it meant someone cared. But I lied and said I had a fall; she knew that I knew that she knew that I had lied. Mrs. Promise was so nice, clearly a channel of the Crimson Light. It saddened me to learn that I had missed the chance to express my gratitude for her kindness, and that was due to a nervous breakdown. She once gave me a 'pass' mark for a test, even though I had been absent. "You are very good at Home Economics, so I gave you a C." Somehow I could not stop thinking, had I sat the test, I could have easily got an A+. I wanted to prove my competence. I resented my parents for not allowing me to be in school that day instead of being on the farm, carrying bananas.

I also thought of the one-on-one discussions of incestuous abuse at the hands of Mr. All-Bags-Full, which at times seemed like a competition. Each sibling would claim her plight the worse. I, especially, felt that way. If they knew my story, even they would agree too. However, I feared hearing, "But really, at that age, you were old enough to know the difference." In fact, those were the very words uttered when I told Yvonne, Mother's eldest daughter, of my experience. Anyway, for this reason, I continued to cloak myself in hiding from my siblings. Many, including those who had an idea, were oblivious to the extent by which these factors had been imposed, far less had they impacted my life.

Things came to a bump approximately three weeks before Mother's passing. I had accepted Yvonne's invitation to St. Lucia; that was after a few months of joyously reuniting with my five-year-old son, Daniel. He had returned from living at the family home on the island. I had just closed down my clothing business after wakening to the fact that my son was my main business. The fact he began calling me Auntie over the phone had sent alarm bells ringing: It was time to handle my responsibility as a mother.

On experiencing a slower pace of life, I began to reconnect with the joys of children's laughter and the smiles of people passing by. I saw flowers beam with colours that had previously gone unnoticed, and then, I missed my loved ones. *I was living on the other side of the coin; the bright side would be my side from now on,* I told myself.

I missed my eldest sister, Yvonne, whom I had not seen in over fifteen years. Yvonne had impacted my life in a big way. I had gathered a lot of my domestic skills from living with her, prior to my trip to the United Kingdom. Though shortly after that, we had an argument, but I felt healed. Our telephone conversation, which also included aspects of our abuse, had reinforced a bond between us, and feeling somewhat elated, I suggested that she visit us in London. To my surprise, Yvonne bluntly refused.

"Why don't you want to come over? I think you would love it here."

She said, "I will not go anywhere that I can't work, unless you can guarantee me work."

That, I couldn't do. Immediately, I felt that my desire to see her was far deeper than hers for me. Putting things into perspective, I valued the Person-Centered theory, to own up my feelings, and in turn, I respected hers, without the imposition of feeling judged or defensive. Then, I was even more surprised by the twist of her next comment, when she offered to contribute to my airfare so that I could meet with her on the island.

"I have already booked my flight; it would be good if you can make it. However, make sure you do not tell anyone that I'll be travelling," she said.

Unbeknown to us, the following two weeks of that vacation would mark one of the most crucial times in our lives.

Yvonne and I spent most of our time together. I got to see her son, Ben, whom I had missed dearly; to some extent, he was like a son I had abandoned. Not only because of the fact that he was perhaps very attached to me in the first two years of his life, but because of the guilt that I had failed to maintain contact with him.

Just two days or so into our vacation, Yvonne dropped the bomb that would commence the battle of our Jericho wall: "My trip here is for a special mission; I did not tell you before, but they better not think I am joking."

"Who are you talking about?"

"Pap and Mom, of course, for all that abuse I went through! They better get me that forty thousand dollars, or they will see. They tell me they don't have money; they better get it. I don't care where they get it from; they'll have to get it! I tell them if they don't give it to me, I will sue both of them."

"Why would you want to sue both of them? I understand with Pap, but Mum?"
"I am holding both responsible."

"But why Mum?" I asked.

"Why Mum?" she repeated. "Because she knew; she knew exactly what Pap was doing all the time."

That conversation quickly ceased from a discussion and became like the six-inch wedged door I had gone through in GPS, leaving me just enough room to back out into a corner. Whoa! I had the sense to hide behind the emergence of thoughts flashing in my mind, without saying much. To sue your parents in London or the United States, for example, was nothing new, but we had never heard of anything like this happening in St. Lucia. That is, despite the fact that incestuous acts had been everyday common dilemmas on the island. As long as I could remember, it was just something people talked about amongst themselves, and that would be as far as it got.

I understood that Mr. All-Bags-Full had impregnated one of his daughters at the tender age of thirteen. I remember missing the big sister; as the eldest one I used to follow around, she was no longer there to bathe me. She was immediately sent away to another district of the island.

The dilemma had left me feeling sympathy for both Yvonne and Mother, even though I felt disturbed about Mother's awareness of what was going on. I still felt that all the demands for punishment should lie on Mr. All-Bags-Full, for abusing his daughters. But why would she have known and not stop him? That was a question simmering on the back of my mind.

There is the belief among some islanders that a man who sleeps with his virgin daughter actually gains power, by rising in the world. This belief extends to other cultures too, and there had been speculation of that sort in this case. Now, if it were a pact with the devil, surely he would have been overpaid, even by one touch, because he was just not worth that much.

As far as it goes, like a shameless case, I once heard a stepfather saying that he would have absolutely no problem sleeping with his stepdaughters, as long as they were over sixteen years of age. What concerned me was that he could not disclose the seduction and enticements involved to gain her trust and to make that happen. Sadly, this truth is denied and overlooked, amongst mothers and caregivers who also, for various reasons, take a rivalry position with the abused individuals. It was hard for me to believe that Mother was so weak or helpless and had perhaps done the same with Yvonne.

Whilst Yvonne appeared focused, I felt that I was put in a very sticky situation, empathising with her yet wishing to exclude Mother and to allow more time for the demand of payment, which was a matter of two days or so. It was not difficult to see that she had given considerable thought to the matter. In the end, I felt it was entirely her decision to make. While I, on the other hand, was not quite ready to let go, I still recognised the echo of my pains.

> You have built for me a wall like Jericho's wall
> But how high are you willing to go, to show that
> You have built me a wall like Jericho's wall?
>
> You've built me a wall?
> Is it six, eight, or ten inches thick,
> As though it was made of bricks?
> Pretending to shelter me from the rain and snow,
> A gesture you thought had entrapped me within!
>
> Have you not noticed the weeds growing
> Through the cracks of that ugly wall that you built?
> And now you are shocked to even hear my voice.
> Yes! Well, it is I, daughter of Zion,
> Conceived by the son of Ray;
> The sun of Light, the Crimson Light.
> Seven times a day I shouted the mournful sounds of the Shophar,
> Seven times a day, regretting my pain,
> But today is your "gain," to tumble down in shame.
> To the thundering steps and sounds of the mighty One.

Alas, even then, it seemed like I was rehearsing just to find comfort: a gain. At least, I had followed on the advice of Paul McKenna: to familiarise myself with the territory that I intend to undertake and overtake, for my gain. I really wasn't ready to tumble down my wall, just because Yvonne was ready. Nonetheless, I would continue my rehearsals, since I knew one day, my wall would be tumbled down and would no longer reign.

I had learnt, from studies of psychology, that life-changing events can impact on our well-being in very profound ways and, in some cases, can actually prove quite detrimental, if not managed well. For this reason, I consciously endeavoured to try to maintain not only a sane mind, but also a sense of stability for my son. Hence, I was unprepared to handle my Jericho wall.

In retrospect, either I was in self-preservation mode or the seed of Actualising Self-full Love had been germinating in me; all I needed, then, was to be gentle with myself. That was despite the chain stitch that was threatening to unravel the fabric of our family tapestry and expose all the naked truths of the ties that bind.

I refused to permit myself to enter into the unknown, as Mr. Altidore seemed to have done. I needed to feel safe, just like the dogs were there for me at GPS, as I ventured into a different sphere in my head, so as to anchor on my sense of protection. Even though I felt that the time would come when I would need to face the fear and one day tumble down my own Jericho wall.

> *"There is no circumstance around you more powerful than the power within you."*
>
> – Iyanla Vanzant

Back at the family home, as I returned from spending time with Yvonne, my appetite for both food and conversation had been in respite. The refusal of either required more energy than to explain the rarity of my saying no to Mother's cooking, so I obliged as she initiated both. Dishing out the food did not permit the air of her usual warmth, as Mother was evidently troubled. Making eye contact seemed to reflect the forceful effort I had made to engage in both food and conversation. The intonation of her voice conveyed a sinking feeling as she spoke.

"I don't see why Yvonne is not allowing the child to come and see me." The statement that conveyed a rhetorical question was enough to mentally engage me. "Ben is my grandson; furthermore, we helped raise him up."

"Did you?"

"Yes! And the others too; they all lived in this house."

"Well, I don't know; maybe because of all what's going on, I suppose."

"It was alright with her when they stayed here, so that she could travel wherever she wanted to go."

Ben was deliberately restricted from visiting his grandparents. Mother was puzzled. "It's so long ago, I don't understand," she explained.

I wanted a light topic, instead of feeling being hit like a tennis ball and forced to choose sides. Part of me just wanted to return to London. In any case, I was really missing my son. Then, I thought, just a few more days until my return date back to the UK, so I will just make the most of my time, whatever shape it may take.

However, listening to Mother made sense that such a case would be the talk of the island and would probably have an immense negative impact on the whole family. At that time, I was not thinking of other people who might have been in the same predicament and perhaps would find the courage to deal with their pain, even raising awareness to those potentially at risk. Mother's reasoning had created more confusion in my mind because of the fact that Yvonne was, indeed, adamant in her quest, and it seemed their only chance for a speedy resolution.

"We do not have that kind of money she's demanding."
I also got a sense from her tone that Yvonne was wrong to make such demand, and she was fishing for my opinion.

"Did you tell sis you don't have the money?"

"Yes, but she said, 'By the hook or by crook, we better get it or else.'"
I was wondering whether Mother was hoping that I could help.
No mind, please don't think that of your mother. She would not. Nah.
If anything, that idea had me to take a look at my position in regards to the matter.
Furthermore, I am not going to be the negotiator, giving the fact I had failed in my attempts to soften Yvonne, I told myself. I felt as though I had become like the six-inch wall, with little else to say, and was happy to welcome the abrupt end of our discussion, as someone demanded Mother's attention we ended with a covert agreement: to be continued.

A wonderful distraction for that contraction.

It was the peak of the school vacation, so the next day, we had a family outing around the island, where we indulged in some of the most beautiful scenery. Our main focus was the volcanic sulphur spring mud bath, located between the twin Pitons of St. Lucia, one of the island's most beautiful and popular sites. I felt tremendous joy flowing through me as I listened to Mother and Aunt Lyle reminiscing and observing the changes that had taken place along the way.

It might have been due to the fact that they had lived only a few hundred yards apart, but I could not recall ever sharing the same proximity with the two women who helped shaped my life so profoundly. The minibus we travelled on was packed, but of course, without Yvonne. I relished in the idea of a perfect distraction of the contractions involving her, yet I wished she could have been there.

I can still recall with delight seeing the young village divers in action, as though they belonged to the ocean. Some were as young as six years old and were diving in several feet of water. They really entertained us. The waters were not only deep, they were so clear that the children would dive to the bottom of the ocean to collect coins that the tourist threw in. Of course, the more coins thrown in, the more the children dived down, and the more money they earned. Apart from that, it seemed like throwing bones to dogs. I also felt that the children were grossly underpaid for their skilled entertainments. Everyone, including Mother appeared so happy, so I quickly decided to remain on the bright side. It made my heart glad to see her happy again.

The sun was setting, and the day's excitement had ended, so we decided to head back home. By then, most of us were tired anyway. After the exchange of a few comments of the day's turnout, most people had fallen asleep.

Unprepared and defenseless against what thoughts I entertained, I replayed my experiences on the island, up until that point. The sisterly bonding, though with some fun, was also challenging. I felt uneasy.

"Is it the incomplete conversation with Mother? It must be the scenario that Sylvia had related as I had arrived on the island."

I began thinking how nice it had been reuniting with Sylvia again after three years, even though this time, it was just for a couple of days. That time when Sylvia, who lived in the Virgin Islands, and I were both on vacation, we had shared the joys of watching our sons take their first steps, in learning to walk, as well as talking about our abusive experiences. I had gotten the feeling we were both making a conscious effort to understand how to deal with our issues. We had discussed the idea of finding a way that would also include Yvonne, in order to help ourselves. We did not follow up on the plan. I suppose this might have been due to various reasons, including the fact that we were still getting to know each other, and especially with the absence of a relationship between Yvonne and me. Going over this thought, I found myself thinking, *How different things might have been if only we had … Done what?* I still don't know.

Sylvia had informed me that just days before Yvonne and I had arrived, things were really bad. She said, "I mean really bad. I just felt something had taken me."

"What do you mean, something had taken you?"
She explained, "I felt something, like something I couldn't control had just taken me. Girl, I went to the kitchen and took a long knife, and I went and pulled down Pap's pants; I was going to cut that off clean! Clean! Clean!"

"Cut what off?" I said, as though needing clarity, but to really be convinced.

"I was going to cut off Pap's penis. I told him, 'Come now! You want to do what you did to me again?' I was going to cut that off and just throw it for the dogs downstairs.

"Girl, if it wasn't for Mum, who held my hand and begged me to stop, I was cutting that thing right off! I would cut it off, I'm telling you."

Perhaps my face was showing disbelief because she kept saying, "It's true! You don't believe me? Ask Mum."

When I turned around to Mother, she said, "Yes, she was going to cut it off, true."

Mother told me that she and Sheba, the youngest daughter, were begging and screaming for mercy: "Don't cause bloodshed," they cried as they tried to pull her off.

Sylvia was still very angry, and I felt that whatever had taken her had not gone far off and was still lurking around.

Now there I was, thinking about all this and Mother's role in our lives. She always seemed to be saving someone. Still, whilst she may have saved some from a few lashes, she had not saved the children from the man, but instead, she saved the man from the child. Sylvia told me that it was to teach our father a lesson, "that was for him to see what it felt like to be vulnerable as I was; when he used to do what he did to me." Now, it's difficult to not try and imagine what it would have been like if Mother had not saved him. I struggled to think that I could actually end up holding his penis, let alone having the detached thing in my hand, and with blood all over. Yet, three daughters had been torn, ripped, and were still bleeding inside. Can the two ever be compared, or are they just flip sides of the same coin?

Nevertheless, I felt a little for Mr. All-Bags-Full, who had already lost one leg to diabetes and, in fact, depended on others for all his basic needs.

I also felt sad for my sister too. "Coin-logically" speaking, I was wondering whether she'd touched on the edge of insanity. However, it might have just been the point before flipping onto the other side, and there is always someone ready to say, "You are crazy!" As much as I tried to see the funny side of that situation, something inside did not allow me the state of sweet laughter that Sylvia had amusingly found. It might have been very different if I had heard the story elsewhere from a different source. Instead, I felt pity for him. I got the impression that Sylvia really just wanted to make a point and would not actually go as far as to cut off his penis. Perhaps yes, perhaps no. Regardless, it was evident that the Jericho wall was cracked and that, of course, was pushing all kinds of emotions up to the surface.

Two days into our vacation, Sylvia returned back to her hometown. In her much typical and unpredictable manner, Yvonne, too, left the island and returned to Canada the following day. That left me three uninterrupted days with Mother.

There was a degree of openness between Mother and I, which was mainly due to the time she spent in my home in London, but subjects of deep nature were not always easy. I wanted to continue our conversation, but it felt like setting up an email account. Although you do not bother to read all the regulations and policies (which nobody does anyway), you become aware of their existence. And also the fact that not until you click "I accept" will you be able to sign in, where you are free to subscribe to gain all sorts of information. The trouble is, with subscriptions, even though you are aware of their nature, you remain oblivious of the *exact* content; that is, until you click "Open." In effect, you have no control of the quality and quantity of information you are being sent, of course, unless you unsubscribe. With eyes open, I did the maths, to ensure my validation for this discussion. Was my point really worth mentioning? That even though Mr. All-Bags-Full did not penetrate me, was my case strong enough? Furthermore, I was also mindful not to be seen as jumping on the bandwagon, where Yvonne and Sylvia had left off, so to speak. The sum tallied: nothing to lose, but your soul to save. So I consented and clicked "I accept."

My first complaint about Mr. All-Bags-Full was still hanging in the air as it resurfaced.

"Mum, I want to tell you that Pap was in the bedroom last night. He was touching me when I was sleeping."

Without turning to look at me, she asked, "Did this happen before?"

"Yes, he was touching all between my legs."

I was left as if waiting to be dismissed after being punished by my teacher.

I believe that Mother had told him off, because shortly after that, he looked at me very angrily (but to look at me in that manner was not uncommon anyway).

Whenever Mother was not around, he would either beat me or pretend to like me, so he could try having his way with me. He often asked a younger sibling to get me to bring him water into the bedroom. On handing it over, he'd ask, "Are you all right?"
I would reply, "Yesss."

Still lying on his back, he would be more occupied with my nipples while intermittently sliding his hand over my shoulders and down my arms instead of taking the glass of water from my hand. Sometimes, it meant making several trips for the day.

However, **I** was again faced with what seemed like Mr. Altidore's smoke-like black hole. *If only I had a flicker of light to find my way through*, I thought. Immediately, I felt a spark of light ignite my powerhouse inside. The Crimson Light was in action, though not ablaze, but sufficient to permit me the courage to ask why.

Once more, we anchored in the kitchen. It's easy to see why the kitchen, with Mother having had fourteen children. Seated at the shining mahogany dining table, I said, "So Yvonne's gone back."

"When did she leave?"

"Today, I didn't even know she was going to leave so soon."

"Uh … She's always like that. She doesn't like people to know when she's travelling."

After a moment's silence, I finally asked the burning question: "Why, Mom, why did you let it happen to us? Why didn't you stop it?"

"I don't know." Still as before, Mother responded and paced back and forth, as a deliberate way to keep busy; she added, "But all that happened such a long time ago, and now you all decide to come with that again?"

"What do you mean, we come with that again?"

"I mean Yvonne; she never stops telling everyone! For so long that happened?"

"Okay, I understand what you're saying with Yvonne telling everybody," I said, because there was the shared view that Yvonne would tell any dog or cat that would listen. "But Mom, because we are affected by what has happened to us, we are talking about it. What I want to know is why you never stopped him before he got to Sylvia and I?"

Mother remained quiet for a while, and as I observed the sad expression on her face, I began feeling guilty for confronting her. It was a feeling that we had exchanged roles; I was her mother and she was my daughter. Then there was the question of respect for your parents. *Have I crossed the boundary?* I wondered, but still with an urgency to proceed: "Mom, I'm feeling dirty and embarrassed, all the time. Especially when I have to listen to people talking how disgusting it is for fathers to sexually abuse their children. Nearly every day, either on the news or at work, I could hear someone saying something as though they know me. I always feel that they are talking about me, even if I know they don't really know me."

After an uneasy pause, Mother said, "All that is happening now, because you all have become too educated."

"What do you mean, too educated?" In other words ignorance is bliss.

"I mean, you all went abroad and listened to what these people are saying, and that is why you are asking me all these questions now."

The allegiance of the Crimson Light must have kicked in straight away. I immediately felt a knot in my gut, followed by a lump in my throat. I was left speechless for a while, as I prayed to hear something that would distract the contraction of my nerves in my head. It had become a case of automatic stillness. I could have refrained from life in that very moment but I also had my son to think about. I felt sad. I felt sad for Mother, and I felt sad for myself. I felt sad for my sisters.

I was still on the edge of the Wheel of Life, hoping to hear something that would help me flip into having a sense of saneness, as Mother continued, "I wanted to protect the family name. The shame would affect the whole family. I did not want to spoil the 'good' family name."

"What difference does it make? As you even said, Yvonne was always telling every dog and cat about it anyway."

"I know."

Well, according to the Bible, "A good name is better than sweet smelling ointment." Now, making the comparisons in my mind, the good name was: "They have a lot of money! Big trucks, big houses, everybody knows them, they are smart, even though sometimes their sons get themselves in a bit of trouble, but they have enough influence and money to bail them out."

Better than sweet-smelling ointment? I thought; the only ointment I knew then was that menthol Chinese oil mixture, with soft candle (specifically formulated for pain), coconut oil, and nutmeg, that had permeated my senses with the daily application of rubbing Grandmother's leg for rheumatism. I did not know how to respond to that, because both name and ointment felt like sickness to me. But I was inclined to agree with Mother, because I had read the text for myself, and the oil smelt bad. In addition, we were taught not to question the scriptures. A command, no doubt, I have broken numerous times, but I find safety in the verse about forgiving the other seventy times seven. And since God is a forgiving God, I would always be forgiven.

What was a good name? I attempted to fine-tune the credentials. The name had earned grand mansions, a track record that had excelled to the "haves" amongst the "have nots," including a string of affiliations to others of influence: the good, the bad, and the ugly. All that seemed a good name? Or wasn't it, perhaps, buying into a sick definition of a good name?

The wheel of fate was spinning, and I was still on edge and wondering whether it was going to be heads or tails for me. I felt like I had been on a high tower and was about to let go. Whilst the idea of letting go offered the chance of completely losing myself, of losing all inhibitions, I was scared. *If I could just scream for a moment*, I thought. Yeah, but how long would I remain in this mental space? What if I begin to scream and can't stop? How would I regain equilibrium? Because, ultimately, it's what my soul seeks.

Where am I now?

Determined to salvage what I could from that discussion, I said to Mother, "So, Mom, are you saying that this is a bad thing that we *know* what happened to us was not right?"

She replied, "No, I am not saying that," still in her usual soft tone.

"Then why are you saying something like that? I don't understand," I said.

"Well, it is not my fault that now I know it is wrong! It's everywhere I go, and some people are being jailed for it; that must mean it is really bad."

The silence, though unpleasant, was finally broken: "Look at me! My father did the same thing to me and my sisters," Mother said, as if to say, "I did not turn out too bad." It was then Mother proceeded to tell me that her father had also impregnated his eldest daughter.

"Well, in that case, that's exactly why you should have warned us, don't you think? Okay, even though it had happened to Yvonne, couldn't you have warned us? You should have told me. Maybe if you had told me, all those things that happened to me in England would not have happened. And why did you have to stay with Pap? You should have left him."

"What could I do, and where would I go? I already had four children by the time I went to London and was pregnant with you. Looking after children on your own is not easy. In fact, that is how I became pregnant with you. Things were hard, and your father used to help me with food; he was always bringing me something." Now, from her storytelling moments, Mother had expressed a sense of independence in London, like having her own savings. However, as I understand it, the economic structure or lifestyle in those days did not foster the means to maintain that sense of autonomy. According to Mother, once married, your husband should support you and the family, anyway.

I became aware that I had been pacing the floor, too. It might have been because I was compensating for the repressed tendency to raise my voice on occasion. I had not wished for another episode of the topic in question, so I consciously covered the main points that caused me concern.

"What about Queen of Sheba?" I said. Though a middle name, a part of me was always envious of the fact that Mother boasted how she had carefully chosen the name Sheba. Furthermore, in my eyes, she looked a real queen. That is not to say that we didn't get along. In fact, we always have, especially after bonding over a whole baked chicken between the two us. It happened that we were so engrossed in conversation that we couldn't be bothered to prepare anything else that day, so we shamelessly ate a whole chicken for dinner. "You have done well to protect her, though?" I asked whilst I struggled to exclude an intonation of sarcasm.

"Well, I always told myself that if he ever, ever made that mistake to even touch Sheba, I would cut his penis off myself."

Now, I don't quite know why, but in that moment, I believed that Mother was capable of making him penis-less. Perhaps she really didn't know how to do better. However, going by her words, Mother still knew enough to put aside her Christianity to make her husband penis-less over Queen of Sheba; I was left confused.

After reviewing my inbox, I unsubscribed. This allowed me to examine the information delivered by my mother. Like pieces of puzzles, I framed the pictures of females of both generations. As I compared the two, it would seem hard to tell who is who because the virus had truly contaminated our lives.

I felt a chill through my bones, with the realisation and extent of this sickness. There was no warmth anymore. Where do I find the courage to look at such ugly pictures? I wondered. The correlation was too scary. Like Mother, Grandmother had four daughters; well, actually five, but one died a horrific death, whilst in her teens. She had fallen off a mango tree and onto a stem that was stuck into the ground. You may be wondering why I am telling this. It is because I find it very difficult to think of my mother's sisters without thinking of this story. Furthermore, I am trying to figure out why Aunty Lyle felt it necessary to tell me then. She said that the stick pierced her sister and had left her as though she'd sat on a stool. *Why are you telling me this, just when I am trying to get some mangoes from the same tree? Furthermore, it is not like I am attempting to climb it anyway,* I thought.

Well, going by my feeling, I can only conclude that her reason was perhaps the same as mine for telling you: a distraction for dealing with pain. A horrible story connected to my favourite fruit, but now I understand that pain and joy are just flip sides of the same coin. I hope, in this case, the joy will somehow come, because where there is one, so too you shall find the other; just both sides of the same coin.

The eldest daughters in both pictures were impregnated by their fathers and were sent away. Consequently, both supposedly had their pregnancies terminated or miscarried. According to Mother, most daughters of both generations were sexually molested by their father, baring one, because the mothers were determined to succeed in the quest to save the one.

Continuing my review, despite all else, I saw Mother as a peacemaker who did not necessarily go beyond bailing out her children from the beatings of her husband and in turn saved him from becoming a penis-less man. Perhaps the way she saw it was "let there be peace, for the sake of the good name." Now, that taught me that whilst our actions or inactions may sometimes lend a degree of peace, it is not without the potential to highlight the cracks of any Jericho wall. My actions, too, had granted a degree of peace that I had actually subscribed to Mother's webpage of the ties that bind. Despite the unfavourable responses, I no longer had that talk on my mental to-do list.

Back in the UK, I happily reunited with my son. I had not followed up my usual habit to call the family, to inform them of my safe arrival home. Instead, I called a day or two later. My second elder brother, Anderson, answered the phone, and I asked to speak with Mother. There was nothing to suggest that she was in grave danger, as he casually explained that she had been hospitalised due to a stroke.

And, in my Chatterbox's attribute, I quickly declared, "Yeah? But she's going to be alright anyway," to which he responded, "Yeah! She'll be alright."

Mother had remained on my mind, every minute, until the following day. It was an easygoing Sunday afternoon with my cousin Veronica and my neighbour Melva. It seemed like an orgasmic eclipse was taking place, as I became conscious of my ability to talk, laugh, listen, and hope, all seemingly at once. I can only assume it was my three separate selves in motion. Everything seemed to be occurring in that single moment. I also became aware that the afternoon summer sunlight was beaming directly on my face, as we sipped on red wine in the lounge. Then the phone rang. I was still laughing on the way to the bedroom, as I was savoring the lingering eclipse.

"Hello, sis," with a solemn voice said.

"You okay?" I responded after recognising Yvonne's voice.

"How can I be okay?" she asked, continuing, "What am I going to do? I don't know what to do."

I said, "How do you mean? Do you mean Mom?"

"Yes, that's what I mean. I don't know if I should go down," she said.

"You don't have to go down; Mom is going to be alright," I said.

"How do you mean, she's going to be alright, when she already dead!"

I screamed with all my might. The loudness and the force seemed to unhinge all my synaptic nerves from my gut and struck my heart. I threw the phone across the room. Melva and Veronica immediately rushed to my aid and asked what had happened. The Crimson Light had blessed me with two of the loveliest people to console me. They were as loyal as the two guard dogs that had waited for me outside of GPS.

By then, all I did was call upon the Crimson Light: "O Gurrrd!" in my highest and the most wimpish pitch, which was due to exhaustion. "God, please make me strong; make me strong like my mother." I repeated this over and over: a prayer that I have come to question its purpose, time and time again, with an inkling of regret, and as many times over. No doubt, periodically, I wrestled in bouts of confusion that compelled me to ask what being strong really means. And on reflection of my mother's life, I sometimes wondered, was it strength or mere ignorance? Yet, equally, I would be expressing gratitude for a much answered prayer, for what I believe being strong means.

Why didn't someone take the initiative, to at least attempt a degree of sensitivity to inform me about Mother's death? Didn't it really matter how I would know? It is necessary that I find the way to forgive others and forgive myself that I never found the voice to tell anyone how I felt, especially Anderson, who has now passed away, it must have been tough on him being the eldest around at the time of Mother's sudden passing as it was for everyone else.

I now choose to forgive myself and all others

For the self-pitiful position I had taken on.

Anyway, there was no doubt in my mind that I would return to the island to be with my siblings and to attend Mother's funeral, and I thanked God that she was not yet in the ground. Because us being together meant the true essence; these are the ties that bind.

Anchoring Points

There are no accidents and no coincidences, but the choices
we make: today I am making a choice to accept
reality,
loss, and
humbleness.

I am now open and receptive to the guidance of the Crimson
Light; therefore, I am trusting the choice I have made to
trust,
initiate, and
examine.

"Underneath the surface appearance,
everything is not only connected with everything else,
but also with the source of all life out of which it came."
– Eckhart Tolle

Chapter Five

Paradox of the Crimson Light

As though following coloured lines painted like those found on hospital floors that unmistakably take one to a waiting room before seeing the doctor, there I was, in the lounge of GPS. I was accompanied by a complete stranger, a middle-aged woman in black. After our short meeting, I had fallen asleep on the red sofa, later discovering the bunch of keys in my hand.

"Why am I here?" I asked, dazzled by the brightest of Crimson Lights that I had ever seen; I felt like being driven on the hairpin bends of St. Lucia's luscious mountains. That was before I had seen the two dogs, the men, including Mr. Barack Altidore, who had stepped into the tombed casket, just like that. Would the light reveal the answers that I sought? Would the keys unlock the paradox of life's mysteries? Would I finally be able to unravel the web that I felt was inhibiting my breath? I couldn't help but wonder about Mr. Barack Altidore; perhaps, like Mother, he did not have a voice? Hence, he was restricted in expanding hidden breath.

Chatterbox's reading had compelled me to focus on the words "This is your life," as I was ready to step into what felt like my own smoky hole. I was delving even deeper. *God knows I needed the light, for the unchartered avenues of my mind would no longer be forbidden*, I thought.

The magnitude of thoughts and memories had got me wondering whether my part of this make-believe movie that I had to act was, in fact, of a dying person. The reason being, it is often said that just before dying, all of a person's life tends to flash right before their eyes. Hoping not to die just yet, but for this reason, it would make sense to consider the flip side of the coin, by unlocking the joyous aspects of my relationship with Mother.

Mother certainly knew how to laugh. In fact, it was a gift that we all have been blessed with. It is no wonder we have a professional comedian in the family. Culturally, and coupled by Mother's unique sense of humour, we are able to see the funny side of most situations. Mother knew how to capture our attention with her favourite pastime, storytelling. In hindsight, it might have been her way to ease our pain from the beatings or divert her attention of Mr. All-Bags-Full whereabouts. "Mom, I want to sit on your lap. No, not you! Me! Me! Meee!' as the younger ones would fight to get as close as possible. It might have been the same when I was their age, but I have no memory of sitting on her lap. Although aloof, I craved for such a moment that I would sit on her lap.

We all laughed at her jokes and listened to the amusing stories, many of which were at the expense of Mr. All-Bags-Full. Our father was not literate and was not the most eloquent speaker in English. So it was always funny listening to him; especially when his high-class friends came to visit. His favourite phrase was, "Yes, sir! Yes, sir! You comprehend me, sir?" It had become the punchline of our giggles, even to this day. Ensuring that we followed the essence of her story, Mother would imitate his husky voice: "You comprehend me?" and we would be in stitches. There was also the story how Mr. All-Bags-Full had called the police concerning a dispute with a young man, called Alfred.

After listening to Mr. All-Bags-Full's complaint, the officer said, "Sir, I understand your complaint, but what would you like me to do?"

Uh-oh. Mr. All-Bags-Full seemed hesitant and repeated his complaint in half-English and half-Creole.

"Yes, sir, I understand, so would you like me to arrest him?" the officer asked.

"Uh-huh, yeah, arress him, but not too hard, okay?"

This carried on for a while, because the officer had not comprehended that "arrest" to Mr. All-Bags-Full meant the degree of physical force imposed, instead of the words that precedes or accompanies the action. Subsequently, the man was not arrested.

Perhaps most popular of all was the "head off or head on" story of Mother's time in England. She had often looked forward to enjoying her fish broth, the sister to the Jamaican fish tea recipe that is commonly served in the UK. Mother said that she often felt thwarted by her inability to understand and to respond aptly to the Irishman's accent at her local fishmonger, who always asked, "Head on or head off?"

Her utterance of "Huh? Huh?" whilst trying to make sense of what she had heard meant her favourite part of the fish would be in the bin: "I would feel sad that I had paid for the head also, but they would always give me a headless fish."

To make matters worse, after a few consecutive trips, the fishmonger had become familiar with her face and specific order, so he would invariably react on the basis of the past head-off order. It was after these unfortunate incidents that she plucked the courage to say, "I want my fish head! What these people think? Don't they know you cannot have tail without head?"

Back in the sixties, the array of fish-head recipes was not so prevalent in the UK; it was perhaps perceived as a poor person's meal, too. The increased migration of black people in the UK, and the quest to maintain the value and cultural traditions, have since created a balance in the use of heads and tails.

Perhaps it is because of the inability to laugh now, but the rays of the Crimson Light still prompt my attention towards Mother's passing and what it really means to me. I just want to be able to balance heads and tails: "You comprehend me?"

I wondered how I was going to survive the wreckage of our Jericho wall. "How would life be for me now that Mother is gone?" My question was encapsulated with guilt and fear, including self-condemnation. "Would I still be considered as part of the family? Or continue to be referred to by some as a 'half' sister?" I had never been akin to the term half-sister, because I felt it required me to behave as half of what I perceived a whole sister to be. That meant I felt half-belonged too. I suppose I felt it gave the impression that I had been grafted with some other organism, like an apple or orange.

Now the main cord to what I hinged on was gone. The thread of the tapestry was unravelling, and the superficiality of that mandatory tie was now perceived as partly mandatory. My inferiority complex, about being the only child in the family with a different father, had squared me in the eye. The thought of feeling belonged, or even whole, had become more frightening, and I was bracing for a potential rejection. I had become used to feeling alone. Thankfully, I was constantly reminded of the Crimson Light, through biblical texts, self-help books, songs, and movies, so that I was really never alone, even though lonesomeness had become my home.

Despite the fact that I did not particularly confide in Mother as a friend, I was faced with the reality of being totally responsible for my emotional well-being without her. The solemn beat that I feared was being played, like a calling to dance to a dreaded tune. It was a dance that I had pondered upon; would my steps wander, or would I simply fall flat on my face? On the other hand, I felt that my time had come; I would prove them wrong, that I can really get on with my own life.

I had danced to the many tunes written for me. However, I also remembered the empowering tunes of the reunion with my son, Daniel. I had not left it to chance, as to when it would be played;

indeed, it was a sweet dance, choreographed by me. Moreover, I felt good about the commitment and sacrifice I had made to give up my clothing business, even though I had no idea what my next move for earning an income would be. But the tunes written for me were now playing louder and louder:

"No, you never gonna make it."

"You never gonna make it if you break my heart."

"Won't make it on your own."

"It's a big world out there."

"You will be nothing in life!"

All that, no doubt, had left me feeling shit scared, very much like waiting for the verdict of Mr. All-Bags-Full's treasure pail. Yet, like then, I was determined to win. As I consciously listened, I realised that I really never had to dance to all the tunes. Other tunes required a sort of stillness for the message to unfold. So, as I listened, I remembered that I came into this world on my own, a fact that I anchored onto, for my relief and sense of self-identity. I was ready to face the words: This is your life.

I had become the child, eager to prove her competence and impress her mother, hoping to get a smile, despite her failings. I wanted to prove that I was able to cope and stand on my own two feet. At a deeper level, as a result, I experienced feelings of guilt that were conceived in a belief that my desire to stand on my own was only attainable through her loss. This led me to ask, "Are we incapable of finding strength unless our dependency is no more?" Did the sentiment of loss become overshadowed by my wish to prove that I can cope well, by myself? I begged for forgiveness. God knows how I yearned to dance to a new beat, one that I loved, and to one day eradicate this tune of hope in my head. I would actually "Get up! Stand up! Stand up for my right" for good, my right to dance to my own tune.

Now on the very day of Mother's funeral, I was listening to other tunes: "Slye and Richard won't be able to attend Mom's funeral, due to circumstances beyond their control," said Anderson. I was really looking forward to all of us being together. That would probably be a first, and fitting too, for this solemn occasion. I could not imagine for one second not attending Mother's funeral. Then I imagined, *It must be quite difficult for them; how will they cope, to not be there?*

I thought of their relationship with Mother: more the end, their goodbyes, you could say. Richard had not visited Mother since he had left the island. I felt especially sad for him. Mother had told me that they had a fight just before he had left for the UK. Richard had sworn that he would never return to visit her. That is exactly what had happened. The evidence of a bitter seed had manifested in full bloom, as an inevitable regret, I imagined. I felt angry that Richard could not be with us, because he had found himself in trouble with the law. Then I was also angry with myself for being angry at him. On the other hand, Slye's excuse had been due to immigration reasons. Now, I felt, if that was me, it would not matter that I couldn't return. I would attend my mother's funeral, I thought. Later, I discovered that there was more to this than I thought.

Why was I angry with Slye for so long? The eldest should have been there for us, I thought. We had been brought to look up to your elders, and he was not there for us. The occasion would also have rendered an opportunity to really face Slye once more. It was as if I was always standing between these two brothers and now to just be left on my own.

Richard and I were particularly close. It was a closeness that derived from lots of fights, mainly instigated by Slye. We fought to keep Slye entertained with his favourite pastime activity. It was just like people who like to watch television at mealtimes, for whatever reason. Slye just loved a good fight. He would egg Richard on to hit me. Richard would push me, until he succeeded in getting me to retaliate which was also prompted by Sly. It was as if we were two roosters in a fighting pen. Richard would be instructed where and how to hit me. And whenever big brother was in the house, you did as you were told. That meant Richard's only motivation was to please him, whilst mine was to defend myself and inadvertently please him, too.

"Let's see who's going to win," big brother would say. Then Richard would land a fist on my arm, "Boop," and I would hit back with a mingy "Bap." **I** did not win, not one single fight. I felt helpless; even though he was nearly two years my junior, he was much taller and stronger than I was.

I never really questioned Richard's loyalty towards me. However, prior to the time of Mother's passing, our relationship was somewhat disconnected. I started opting out; our usual scenarios:

"Sis, you got a little change?"

And I would say, "How much?"

But when one day, I said to him, "Bro, can you punch this guy for me?" he said, "What for? I can't hit the guy just like that."

"Why not?"

"I can't just hit the guy, and I don't know why I'm hitting him."

"Because I just asked you."

By then, I was not only losing my fight with the young man, but also my sense of reasoning with my brother. I didn't get it, that he actually refused to hit the young man. I did not feel that this was working for me, like almost everything else at the time. I felt that I was always available for others, but they were not there for me. Even at twenty-two, I had not understood this simple equation that one needs to elicit enough aggressive emotion, to participate in an act of violence. After all, that's how he and I used to fight: Boop! Bap! Boop! Boop! And before I could slip another Bap, I would feel Boop! And it would be game over.

Furthermore, my naivety to gather much sense, even around the beatings from Mr. All-Bags-Full, did not help. In hindsight, I realised that I had gained enough of the stuff to bulldoze the young man head-on, and all by myself. Even then, thankfully, though unaware at the time, the Crimson Light was hovering over me. I only knew something was wrong. As it happened, the thread of our relationship seemed to be thinning. Needless to say, we were both trying to find our paths in life.

Anderson had taken on board the funeral arrangements, and no doubt he was the best person for the role. As well, he was the eldest around. He was not only very educated, but he was also a very charismatic man, God bless his soul. Anderson was confident and was a very assertive young man, with skills gained as a farmer, agriculturist, and teacher. In addition, his range of interests gained him the privilege to travel to various countries, including Asia.

Funerals on the island can be lavish events, depending on how one is perceived, in respect of what they stood for in their community. Things like that would determine the number of attendees at your funeral, unless the "stayers," meaning family members, requested otherwise.

I wrestled in my mind to fully absorb the sinking in of Mother's passing and why she died. There was no doubt in my mind that the pressures of threats from Yvonne, talk about the cutting of the penis from Sylvia, and the probes for answers from me caused Mother's death.

Sylvia kept on saying, "I want to know what killed Mom. I want to know the cause of Mom's death."

I thought, *What are you going on about? Anyone can do this simple equation.*

However, it had been entrenched in my mind that Sylvia had always been the brighter one; in addition, I did not want to make matters worse, so I kept silent.

"I think Mother died of hypertension," Sylvia said.

Dah! I thought to myself. And yes, Mother had been treated for hypertension, for a number of years, but likewise, for a long time, she had also followed a healthy lifestyle plan, particularly around food and nutrition. She studied many books in her spare time on alternative medicines, including general healthcare advice. And she often shared her skills and knowledge with people around her. She even became a vegetarian and was also very creative with foods. In fact, Mother was the first person that I knew to make pumpkin bread, a demonstration of her diverse range of creativity.

Preparing for the funeral in itself had a degree of excitement because of the constant flow of people in and out of the house, conveying their condolences. Others offered their support in preparing wreaths and foods of various kinds. Behind the house was the slaughtering of animals, something I had not witnessed for about eighteen years. Somehow, I had to make a conscious decision to not dwell on the fact that I felt sorry for them. Everyone seemed occupied in some way, even if that meant engaging the visitors in conversations. I got the sense that the orchestration of the event, in itself, was meant to either divert our attention away from the intense solemnity of our loss or the adverse: to drill into our heads the reality that "Your mother is dead."

That, in turn, also presented the question "How should I behave?"

The impact of that thought did not allow time for superficiality, as I drifted into the reminiscence of my youth. It was somewhat like preparing for the Sabbath, where we would sing praise of devotion to God, but with the exception that Mother's eternal day of rest was much grander. On Fridays, we had to prepare, well before sunset, the commencement of the Sabbath. Only this occasion, we were not racing against time. We were always rushing, doing things that were not of the Lord's, even well after sunset. I took on my former role once more to iron the clothes to be worn to church the next day.

Pressing with our first electric iron, in hindsight, I realised was a detrimental novelty.

Consequently, I would endure a series of shocks, with my arm being pulled by the current; I would be thrown onto the next side of the room. It was just like the fights between Richard and me, with the exception I was always determined to win. Therefore, I would endure that modern-day technology device instead of the traditional iron that was heated up on burning charcoal in a clay coal pot. I did so until I became immune to the shocks, since not only was it easier to control the temperature, but it also lessened the risk of dirtying the white clothes from the cinders. I used to think, *Were it not for the good intention of ensuring everyone well-groomed for the Sabbath, I'd be dead by now.*

I was now able to relish in the reality of a safer experience, physically. My emotions, on the other hand, reflected the paradox of the Crimson Light: Since I had endured the shocks, I would be able to endure Mother being finally laid to rest. I would be strong. As I also found myself consolidating my ironing experiences, it gave me a chance to see how I contributed to my siblings turning out well-groomed for another day of rest: Mother's Sabbath.

Eventually, the corpse arrived. In that moment, everything seemed to be slowly turning upside down by various synchronistic murmurs. In that moment, the sounds of intonations seemed to be the force controlling the movements of the undertakers. I got a feeling that people expected you to behave a certain way, and the only way is to bawl. I was determined not to gratify their wish even though I could not conceal my tears.

I had seen dead people before, but none of them had been my mother. Without any hesitation, I yielded to the force and bowed my face next to the cold corpse; I was certain that she wasn't there.

We headed for the church and discovered that the funeral service was being conducted by a group of pastors who, for various reasons, were quite close to the family.

"Brothers and sisters, we are gathered here today, on this very sad occasion of our dearly departed sister … We are deeply sorry for the loss of wonderful wife, mother, and friend. We would like to extend our most sincere thoughts and prayers to her husband … and all her children, including the two who, sadly, are not able to be with us …"

This was nothing like Chatterbox presenting Mr. Barack Altidore's eulogy. The church was full and could not accommodate everyone, and though I was taking in the service, I couldn't miss the spirit of people moving around and trying to perhaps get closer.

"Our sister … was like the true virtuous woman referred to in Proverbs, chapter 31," one pastor commenced. Those of us who knew her well felt that to be a fact, because anything but virtue seemed inconceivable and otherwise difficult to accept. It felt really good to hear so many wonderful things being said about my mother.

In my heart, however, though not quite like Chatterbox, I was adding to but could not subtract from what was said.

Mother was a loving, kind, and very generous woman, who got up early in the morning to do her best by ensuring meals were cooked, laundry was done, and our clothes were stitched in time. She was very hard working, and apart from being a seamstress, she also worked as a cook for the men who were employed by her husband, either on the road or on the farms. Mother knew how to satisfy their palates and their bellies, as she did us, with delicious meals that are still spoken about to this day. That, in turn, provided her an income by which she maintained her home.

Despite having fourteen of her own children, Mother often took in other people's children; for whatever reason, she'd have them around. With young and old friends alike, nothing was ever too much or too little to share.

However, there was a part of me that was simply itching to reveal what nobody else could but I: the secret I held deep inside. How the impact of Mother's virtuousness had blighted my sense of judgement.

Maybe it was the love, maybe it was the shame, but this I had visited time and time again. "You have to understand that you were born in sin, and according to the Bible, that makes you a bastard! Not until you accept the kingdom of God, and its righteousness, by repenting of your sins will you become God's child. If not, you will still belong to Satan."

I was shocked to be called a "bastard" by my mother, even though I had never checked the dictionary meaning until then. I knew it from the time I spent in London; it was only used to insult and disrespect and downgrade the sense of humanity in society.

"Are you saying that I am a child of Satan, even though the Bible says that we are all created in God's image and likeness?"

"Yes, it's right here in the Bible!"

I refused to even look at what Mother was pointing me to read. My confusion lay with the fact that I felt Mother had refused to entertain any common sense, in this context. Yet she was unafraid to explore the teachings of different faith schools, even though it would be unthinkable amongst many of her church members. Her spirit of condemnation tore my heart with her words; they had also made me wonder who really needed to repent, and why?

"I suppose that I am the only born sinner?" I asked.

"No, because the Bible says that we are all born sinners, but I have already repented. Because you were conceived in adultery, you should repent."

Now, since I had never met anyone who was proud to be Satan's child, I had to find out how and where, exactly, I stood in life's equation. No matter how I looked at it, I still would not have entered the kingdom because I was oblivious of my participation in the act of my confinement. There was another point raised: Can anything good come out of bad? I was not only born in sin, but in adultery also. I was not just an ordinary sinner.

As a result, and for some sort of identity, I reinforced my early teachings and beliefs of Catholicism that, I felt, at least it offered hope. It also granted the chance for some kind of resolution, for feeling caught between heaven, hell, and purgatory. I always felt that heaven was far beyond my reach. Consequently, I was left with the battle between hell and purgatory. Equally, I never saw myself as so bad that I would actually end up in hell; I was never that wicked. Therefore, I found some comfort in purgatory. It was to me like Hope for the People. Purgatory is somewhere you stay till God decides what to do with you. This learning had been my confirmation and was taken very seriously, too.

In my heart, I would try and be a good person. God would feel sorry for me and allow me time, even to get a C grade. And I would end up in heaven, eventually. I discovered through this journey that, more than anything else, I would like to lay down this issue and allow it an eternal Sabbath, just like Mother was laid into the ground.

After the funeral, Anderson called a meeting: the first, apart from the usual nights of devotion, which had ceased to exist for me. It reflected the motto: "The family that prays together, sticks together," because, then, we were together.

Everything went well without a hitch; everyone's spirit was temperate. We happily reminisced about the event and acknowledged the grand turnout of a very popular woman, as though we were patting ourselves on the back. As we all gathered in the once-coupled bedroom, Anderson's voice conveyed a degree of sensitivity that seemed to acknowledge each individual's heart for their concern of missing not only their mother, but also their brothers.

"We are sorry that Richard and Slye are not with us in person, but their presence is still very much felt," he said, "and even at this very moment. We know that had it been possible, they would be with us, as they have sent everyone their deepest sympathy."

I felt a layer of warmth around my heart, in just the tone of his voice. Anderson proceeded to give the breakdown of the funeral expenses. It sounded absurd that it should cost so much when one dies.

He asked our father, "How much money have you got to contribute to this amount, so that we can finish paying the undertakers?"

"My chiren, I doh av much money lef," he said. "Just before you-all modar die, we had to make a big payment;" and he continued to explain that what was left was all tied up in other ventures.

Anderson asked, "So is there an insurance policy?"

"I only have about three ..."

Whatever the figure that Mr. All-Bags-Full had uttered, in that moment, I just remember doing the mental arithmetic that equalled "Not worth mentioning." I had to quantify my findings:

"Two mansions and trucks, including lands, and you don't have money to bury your own wife? Where does that fall into the equation? I certainly cannot work this one out!"

The question for payment was redirected to us, the children. "Where are we going to get the balance of nearly forty thousand dollars?"

We were brainstorming, with limited answers. Then all of a sudden, Yvonne announced that she had forty thousand dollars that she could lend us, but we must pay it back. So we arrived at a solution: Each adult would pledge the amount which he or she could repay. Yvonne also offered a generous amount of ten thousand dollars, as her contribution.

Now, because of Yvonne's general seriousness in such matters, those of us who pledged knew very well to honour our agreement with her. As much as we were amazed that she actually had this large sum available, we were equally impressed that she had saved the day. At least, it still left us with some dignity. Our precious family name would not be jeopardised, especially with the undertakers.

I don't know why on earth it took me that long to do this simple arithmetic. Perhaps it is because there was no prior need to observe the direct correlation with the monies demanded from our parents and the loan offered to us. Can it be that death makes one so blind? To think that you could miss something so simple, for so long, right before your eyes? Chatterbox had certainly got me going where I once dreaded.

Now there was another crucial tune still to be played. The younger children were asked to leave the room, just as I had caught myself thinking, *I wonder what he might be feeling*. I could not help but notice Mr. All-Bags-Full seated on the bed; we had all formed a semicircle around him, as though he was Yule Brenner in *The King and I*, and there I was, half wishing it were not so. Yet I felt sad for him.

As a remaining attendee, I still held onto my seat on the floor, near the entrance: It had been my conscious act for half-wanting to be there and perhaps seeking the attention to be coaxed further inside, so that I would get a real sense of belonging.

Then the last item on the agenda was the family secret truths, revealed. Anderson confronted our father about having sex with his own daughters, which Mr. All-Bags-Full admitted doing. That's a relief, I thought, because I knew of another who said, "No, it wasn't me." Expressing contempt for our father's behaviour, Anderson sternly reprimanded Mr. All-Bags-Full, as though they had, in fact, exchanged roles. Anderson was clearly the father, but not with the characteristics of the man whom he was facing, whilst Mr.

All-Bags-Full, on the other hand, was perhaps wishing that he was the man Anderson had become.

Anderson said that he could not understand a father could do such a thing to his own daughters.

"Unthinkable," he said. "That is not how a father should be with his daughters. In fact, you are supposed to protect them, not have sex with them."

When I heard this, I developed a sickening feeling and attempted to get out of the room, but with big brother's stern demand to remain there, I stayed put. I was not ready to look at the string of incestuous abuse cases that I had encountered, and I was definitely not ready to look at this one. In any case, I felt I had enough to think about, including my conversations with Mother. Moreover, this was not my preferred way of handling things. If Mr. All-Bags-Full had been put on the spot, so was I, even more.

I had been learning to trust my process, and what was happening just did not feel right to me. It might have been because I had not been informed about what was to take place. As I listened, there were all kinds of mixed feelings going on inside me. I was in the paradox of my brother standing up for me and also being faced with the eruption of anger and pain that accompanied that case. Anderson was also very angry of the fact that he had been painted with the same brush.

He said that people were saying, "Like father, like son," which meant he was being accused of the same crime. It is not a nice feeling for people to paint you with the same brush of somebody else's crime. He did not feel it was fair that "the sins of the father should fall on the son."

Naturally, Yvonne and I had wondered about that story, which she did not believe. I was very concerned whether it was true that Anderson would ever do such a thing. In the end, I felt relieved to be able to confirm my belief that he would not do such a thing.

After highlighting the father's sins against the daughters, the sinner bent his head in full of acknowledgement of his crime.

He said, "My sins have found me out, and I am glad that God has permitted me to face them today, and I am asking you all for forgiveness."

He also made special mention to acknowledge me as his own. Since forgiveness is one of God's requirements of us, I felt that I had been presented an opportunity to get nearer to purgatory.

"I forgive you," I told him. Then I realised that the acceptance that I was seeking had constituted the line that Mr. All-Bags-Full had just cast: "Forgive me."

Maybe that acceptance had also given me the chance to explore the pain and resentment that I had been carrying because of him. It's like being in an accident and feeling it's your fault, with a total denial of the impact of your injuries. I had trivialised the magnitude of the damage just to cope and hope it would go away. Furthermore, due to the many cases I had pending, I had not considered that as a road-maker, the act of abuse had also opened a pathway that signalled a "through road," with all potentiality for a highway.

This confusion had also left me wondering, where am I on the spectrum of abuse and healing? That meant I would have to consider HFTP to fully recover and make it my sanctuary for purgatory.

I had danced to Mother's tune, trying to identify with her, as she perhaps did with her mother: accepting a mentality enmeshed in a paradoxical concept of love, a love that becomes so hard to define, that often the petals of the rose are missed and all one feels are its thorns. By that, I was able to understand that this is the very sentiment responsible for people remaining in unhealthy relationships and a way of carrying the baton that continues its existence onto other generations. I had become like a puppet swinging on the pendulum of emotions. And at that point, all I did was to maintain my smile that would convey to the world that "everything is alright." But one can only smile for so long, while they're being pricked by the thorns or enduring the ugly scars cause by the thorns.

As I look back, I was also able to see the petals that had fallen onto the ground and been trampled upon. It was her gentleness I felt; in the middle the night, Mother was tucking me in on both sides. Though trying not to wake me up, I opened my eyes to the warmest smile that I knew. From here on, I would follow the long-trailed fragrance of the rose petals of her smile.

Picking up the petals had caused me to see their optimum beauty was not without the thorns. And what I was now experiencing was their true characteristics, through sensations of heaviness and bouts of lightness and relief. The heaviness was a realisation of the weight that I had been carrying through a catharsis, long awaiting to be released: my pain, and the loss of Mother. The lightness and relief had derived from intervals of the emotional release, which, in turn, created a shift in my consciousness.

The shift had reflected my position of being mothered and being a mother. Twice, I asked myself, *How can I do better?* The first time had prompted me to do the right thing, when I decided to reunite with my son. I wanted to avoid the comment, "I wish you were there; why did you send me away?"

The second time, I had to find a way to deal with the pain that I had indeed caused: "I wasn't there because I had sent you away." As those words were bashed against my ears and the teardrops trembled, in them, was a reflection of my strength in Daniel, then ten years old. All I could hear was "This is your life." I could no longer hide.

What else could I have said: "I did the best I could then, for sending you away."

I became conscious that the Crimson Light seemed to shine on each teardrop, as though ensuring me of its presence, so I could continue to look into corners of my mind. Yes, I was sick, I had to admit, but with the strength that I could only have gained from Mother, I still found love through unravelling the yarns of the family tapestry.

When Mother died, she left with me all I knew to be true, including all inexplicit truths, that were once hidden by layers of guilt and shame. The truth no longer remained disguised by hierarchical positions and pompous façades. This truth could not remain eternally hidden: The kind of truth that finds its place to germinate that which would ultimately bring forth after its kind. Like a seed in the ground, it continues to present opportunities for shedding of old skin. Whose skin? one may ask. The one needing to lay down his burdens onto the ground. Perhaps a red rose in bloom, including its stem of thorns, because to lay all is to surrender to the Crimson Light, which is all pure petals and thorns, alike.

This is exactly like having my child, I thought.
The truth of the daily laying down of myself to foster life;
A dying of pride, just to provide, whilst enduring shame and guilt,
Just to ensure the commitment of life's gain is reached.
No matter the case, I would pursue my solemn
oath to my dependent; my loving child.
This I would do, and even to the very end.
In essence, it's about knowing when to protect;
When to nurture; and to love implicitly;
And have the wisdom to discern, when
all others become secondary.

Then I wondered, was my mother's stroke, her solemn oath,
As to provide the love that she held so deep inside?
As I seek for the answer in all explicit truths;
Laid scented petals in the patterns of my mind,
Shining through the Crimson Light
I anchored on the paradox of Mother's smiles:
Now, a red rose in bloom, from the corner of my eyes,

The brightness of the petals had somehow found a way;
That for as long as I live, I would recognise Mother's love,
I wish to convey even through my smile.
Perhaps deep down in her heart, she always knew that I could,
To not only stand on my own two feet, but
I would unravel the mysteries;
By unstitching the yarns and tearing apart,
The event that constitutes the paradox of life;
And perhaps one day, our eyes will behold
a bright and strong tapestry,
Where we can joyously say, "These are the ties that bind."

Therefore, since I intend to hand over the
baton of strength even before I die,
Let it be said, it was a race well run. Since I no longer hide,
I can't help but think that perhaps, it was
also Mr. Altidore's intention,
To have carried forth his oath, by handing me the baton,
So I, too, can confidently tread the paradox of life,
By picking up the red petals, so I could find my peace,
A peace that would resonate within me, as seeds,
Through which I now see that Mother's kindness
Had allowed me to enjoy a most wonderful sleep,
One just like I did on the red sofa in GPS.

The instinct and love, in what a mother displays,
Is so often muddled by our immature vision;
Of which, its development is so vital to ignite
The pureness of what she truly portrays.
That, in itself, induces deep sleep, until
one is ready to be awakened.
All those events were now no longer my smoky black hole.
And now, I am up, by the brightness of the red rose in bloom.
The aroma so divine; I thank God I can
breathe. Therefore, I will succeed.

Such an enriching experience,
I could swear the beautiful mountains
on the island were sculptured,
Even out of its fragrance; right here!

Yes! I can now breathe and even expand my breath,
As I seemed to have found the use of the keys
Which helped me unlock Mother's love alright,
But it was not without entering through the doors of HFTP
And to experience the paradox of the Crimson Light.

Anchoring Points

There are no accidents and no coincidences, but the choices
we make: Today, I am making a choice to cherish
life,
experiences, and
newness.

I am now open and receptive to the guidance of the Crimson Light
therefore; I am trusting the choice I have made to recognise
sacredness,
strength, and
love.

"I realise that I have created this condition
And I am now willing to release the pattern
In my consciousness
That is responsible for this condition."

– Louise L. Hay: *You Can Heal Your Life*

CHAPTER SIX

Guilty as Charged

Though I had taken a series of therapeutic interventions, read a lot of self-help books, got baptised twice as a born-again Christian, I felt incomplete for the journey to the Bridge of Actualising Self-full Love.

Why am I here, feeling guilty as charged? Guilty! It had taken me so long to figure out why I was there, to see Mr. Barack Altidore stepping into the tombed casket, just like that. Guilty! I had overlooked the magnitude of my hurt and the guilt of my need to revisit the scene of the crime, so that I could stop feeling guilty as charged.

I felt as though I had broken every law and was forced to consider the "Thou Shalt Not" laws. Perhaps that is why "law" is a word that I never really liked. Law, I believe, is all to do with the first movie I had watched as a child, at the age of thirteen or so: *The Ten Commandments*. The biblical story tells how a forty-day journey to the land of Canaan, promised to the children of Israel, had turned out to be forty years of misery and pain. God had given Moses, the leader of the tribe, a set of laws to straighten up his unruly children. Adding to my feeling was also the belief that the free entry for viewing the movie, given to pupils at the time, was a deliberate ploy intended to counteract children's rebelliousness, just like the Israelites.

Consequently, that experience served as the foundation for learning that law constitutes every lesson taught and, subsequently, every lesson learnt. It's either the law of the land or the law of gravity or the law of relativity that makes all one's actions constantly governed by law. However, I seemed to have been gravely affected by the raw primary Mosaic law, intended as love, and instead, I gained heaps of guilty charges. It was so, even in my endeavour to implement the refined version, through the law of Christ, to love myself and to love my neighbour as myself.

This led me to examine two interrelated laws, by which I hoped, with clear understanding, to have all my guilty charges dropped. I think it's about the way they were presented that made them so appealing: the law of equilibrium and the law of attraction. Now, why the law of equilibrium? I simply believe that it's the vivid image of the vintage scale that my Aunt Lyle used in her grocery shop that still remains with me.

I use to pride myself in my ability to gauge, very closely, the exact amount of sugar, or flour, or whatever weighable items that the customer had requested. There were times, too, when I enjoyed the sound created by the impact of the two iron points knocking together. Then, I would further indulge in the process of taking off the excess item, until I got it right. The customers' common expressions of frustration, "Hurry! Hurry up, I have to go!" would often reduce me to allowing them the excess. It was so, particularly, when the comments were uttered in a tone that caused me to feel incompetent. However, there was often the chance of a payoff: a smile in return.

Other times, when I insisted on getting it right, I would risk being labelled "can't weigh right" or "don't even know how to weigh." Nevertheless, I would shield myself in my position of importance: the more powerful side of the counter, even with my head barely reaching above it. In retrospect, I believe that ever since my days in Aunt Lyle's shop, I have been in constant battle, trying to gauge myself on the scale of life's equilibrium. Moreover, the periodical balance is not without life's hard knocks.

Now, I like the law of attraction. Perhaps it's simply because I find the word "attraction" attractive, and therefore, it seems to soften its sub-main law. You see, sometimes when you can't really avoid an issue, you just need to find the most susceptible point, in which to make it lighter or more appealing to accept. That's what I did. And I believe that my active participation of this approach is what has brought me on this journey to actualise self-full love. Therefore, I affirmed:

> Dear Crimson Light,
> I may not have always been attentive to walk in your path,
> For it is often said, man prefers darkness to light.
> I recognise that I am surrounded with stacks of guilty charges.
> It's my desire to feel lighter
> And to get onto the Bridge of Actualising Self-full Love.
> I now open my eyes that I may see
> The Light that guides my steps
> And to have all my guilty charges dropped!
> Let it be so.

I realised that often, in my experience, there seems to be a way of doing and being that works well. I am guessing when this happens, it means that one is intentionally following the laws and principles necessary for the desired outcome. For instance, if you were baking a cake, you could expect the same results for each subsequent procedure (providing, of course, you have applied the exact principles and ingredient each time; that is, including the applicable oven temperature). However, this may seem to cease in its effectiveness over time. For example, one day, you discover that your cake didn't rise. To find out why, you go over the procedure, and you are certain that you have done everything right. You examine the ingredients and all the labels of your packages; they are the same as before, the same products and brands. You think to yourself, perhaps the rising agent has passed its-used by date, or there was a fault with the manufacturer. Despite that possibility, you still blame yourself by thinking you must have done something wrong; it's all your fault. That's exactly how I felt before experiencing the timely series of events that led to my witness of Mr. Altidore's descent into the tombed casket, just like that.

My soul was seeking balance on the law of equilibrium. My mind was seeking to understand what I was attracting into my life and why. Consequently, I was further issued a conviction that stated, "Guilty as charged."

Now, principally, in the case of your nonrisen cake, the law of attraction would support the idea that, despite feeling disappointed, your experience was the result of the attention that you gave your intention. That, in turn, had overridden your concern for baking a perfect cake. That meant, what you were resisting had persisted up until that point, of course: the lessons to be learned. Perhaps it was your desire to know just how you would handle such a disappointment amongst your friends, simply because it had happened to someone you knew.

"Unbelievable!" you might say. Well, there you have it, handed to you on the scale of the law of attraction; thus, according to Lisa Nichols, "The universe had only 'downloaded' your request." The energy that had been applied had, in fact, matched its persistence on the scale of the law of attraction and, as a result, would establish equilibrium in it manifestation. That is not to say, however, that everything manifested is in direct balance for an overall, healthy lifestyle, of course. Hence, the predicament I was faced with, for attaining balance.

Therefore, I wondered what underpins the workings as to why some desired items were being downloaded, whilst others were not.

Why, so often in my endeavour to achieve my goals, do I tend to collect even larger amounts of guilty charges? To find out why, I became an investigator. The thought of going down memory lane to Auntie Lyle's shop immediately generated sensations of butterflies in my gut. *Perhaps the answer that I am seeking is right there,* I thought. That, in turn, presented the fear that in order to argue my case, I would need to prove that I can indeed weigh right.

The lonesome return to Aunty Lyle's shop brought back lots of happy memories, as well.

Aunty Lyle was perhaps the most easy-going person I knew. It might have been exactly why she did not rake in a huge profit, but nevertheless, she has never gone without. Regardless of that fact, I felt in my mind a need to take comfort in the warm glow that had hovered over me, as an assimilation for guidance and protection, in which I would gain enough strength to look at the past.

Remembering is good, although painful at times, but good.

I remembered the golden principle: to always express gratitude. In that moment, a sensation of awe came over me, in appreciation for the opportunity to explore my intention, despite my position as one in detention. I was determined to find the good, even in that very situation. *I would have all my guilty charges dropped and be on my way,* I told myself, and I continued to give thanks to the Crimson Light:

"Crimson Light, I thank you for your presence,
For staying with me; and guiding me;
And lighting up my path.
Amen."

I imagined how great I would feel to have my path brightly lighted before me and thought that I would devote my energy to maintaining the good feeling of lightness, not only inside, but all around me. Then, I remembered Bishop T D Jakes, on *The Oprah Winfrey Show*. He said, "It's not because something makes you feel good, that it necessarily means that it must be good for you." He also said that when it comes to decision-making, we should not make our choices based on our emotions, because our emotions often lead us into making the wrong choices. On that basis, I could not argue against the general repercussions of hedonistic and other self-destructive behaviours, such as jealousy and revenge, which are evident in everyday living. However, I thought, surely, not even the bishop would argue against one making a decision based on the desire to feel light of emotional charges. After wrestling with these two perspectives, I must say I was beginning to feel like a nonrisen cake. Shouldn't the same principle work each time? I wondered.

Now, as far as I am concerned, for the most part, my feelings certainly have served me well. From my formative years, and even up until now, happy or sad, they continue to guide me. My feelings have alerted me of hunger, anger, thirst, shelter and protection, love, hurt, and even where to get an available parking space (which also includes the feeling of exultation that accompanies the "Yes!" exclamation of my success).

On the other hand, I can see how certain emotional inferences, from parental influence to societal conditioning, would be considered unhealthy in decision making. For instance, some of my primary and secondary trainings taught me that my feelings were not to be trusted and that I needed to rely solely on others for my development in the world. That meant parents, for example, introduced the assistance of providing three square meals per day, which dictated when I should be hungry, and schools, on the other hand, introduced my bathroom break times, and that dictated when I used the bathroom.

Then, I made the decision to obey the commandments that were not consciously based on my internal values but, rather, others' values, mainly based on the fear of rebellion. It was so, until I decided that others had too much control over me. Therefore, I exerted restraint against what I felt had been indiscreetly imposed upon me, as theirs versus mine (although I do admit I am not sure that I could ever fully distinguish one apart from the other). You could say, I had become deeply engrossed in a game that involved the interchange of external and internal principles as values. That game, in turn, became the instrument for supplying, on demand, guilty charges. Some I attained through learning how to speak; how to laugh in different environments; how to eat in public and cry at funerals. Of course, on the latter, I graduated with honours.

Evidently, some applications worked better than others, whilst I struggled with the rest. Regardless, the result I often felt manipulated, in order to bring about what was required of me. Therefore, I was shouted at so that I could feel embarrassed enough to avoid a reoccurrence of others' discontent. I would be beaten so that my skin would burn enough to generate a sense of wanting to please others the next time round. On this basis, to be told that it is not wise to make decisions based on my feelings, pardon me, but it does sound confusing. I mean, it was through feeling-based conditioning that I was able to satisfy others.

Likewise, the same dis-ease of feeling made me want to rid myself completely of guilty charges. You can understand how this learning had left me in a constant battle of suppressing different feelings and emotions, whilst yet embracing others along the way. As I grew older, in various stages of my development, I struggled with the battle of knowing which emotion to suppress, repress, or exhibit. That would also depend on what actions others had a handle on, or how strong or determined or rebellious I became. In other words, whatever seeds were being sown in me, and my receptivity, determined the outcome.

My feelings and emotions have been for me the drug that highlights the confusion of limitations, satisfaction, and dissatisfaction (LSD), whether they reflect as good or bad, subtle or intense. I just know that my feelings always said something, whether I understood what was being conveyed or not. In this case, it would not be difficult to see why my emotions, under such circumstances, could be perceived as unhealthy for making sound decisions. After all, I would score quite low on the scale of equilibrium for a healthy life.

On the other hand, how else would I have learnt how to develop or distinguish my sense of internal values that summed up "there should be a law against hurting me like this, because that doesn't feel right"? Parental and societal values often claim, "We know what is good for you. Good things never feel nice. Just like medicine, 'the bitterer, the better!'" Perhaps their manual for life, which heralds many biblical principles, had handed me an even greater implication in my development as an individual. Consequently, that was exactly what resulted as my LSD. For instance, I felt inferior inside as I tried to adjust in the community. And that seemed to fall in direct correlation with what the bishop said: "God is not really concerned with our emotions, but rather, what is good for us." That is why I felt that my internal values didn't matter so much; after all, they know best. Now, that was the general view of what held the structures of my experiences. Then, I embarked upon these words:

> Practice make perfect.
> You are free to believe what you choose
> And what you do attests to what you believe.
> Let us be glad that you will see what you believe
> And that it has been given to you to change
> What you believe.
> – Helen Schucman, *A Course in Miracles*

My thoughts and beliefs of my inability to identify my internal values from my external values had made it increasingly pressing to find a solution. Now we are learning that if one practices how to listen well, she can actually, through the state of mindfulness, identify her feelings and thoughts apart, and even trace them back to their derivative state.

I did not learn this stuff when they were beating the crap out of me and forcing me to count the number of each lash, not only at home but also in school. In any case, it would perhaps be impossible to do the maths, whilst trying to make an observation, by which to ascertain whose values matter, as what is yours and what is mine. But is this not where the real challenge lies: in how to not only assemble and disassemble but also reassemble our thought and feelings, in order to be able to make sense of our world?

It seemed like the law of attraction was playing a game and was determined to teach me a lesson as I was served a cup of tea down memory lane.

The young man said, "Would you like sugar?"
"Yes, please," I said.
"How many? One? Two?"
"One, please," I replied.

His politeness reminded me to express gratitude once more, and that made me feel good. Was I being mindful? I often entertained this question, as though I was under surveillance. What is mindfulness? I wondered. Instantly, I back-tracked my mind-movie and pressed Play: *Making a Cup of Tea.*

A simple sentiment, of making a cup of tea, one might think. Oh no, it's much more than that. In my kitchen, as I plugged in my new kettle, I felt privileged for the use of electricity. On the kettle was written, "Made in China." The box and packaging might have been provided by another company, still made in China. Someone else had the job to ensure that it had passed the health and safety checklist before being shipped thousands of miles away. Of course, it was further handled by a line of people: loading and off-loading until it was neatly placed on the shop shelf, in my favourite colour, and with a price tag that saved me asking, "How much?"

The sugar and the teas were cultivated in the Caribbean and had undergone a similar procedure: offering the choice of not only various colours and strengths, but flavours too, and endeavouring to meet my taste buds. Thus, I was able to experience the evidence of the steps and procedures that were put in place to ensure their safe consumption. The smoothness of the rim against my mouth was the realisation that one can't go wrong being mindful, as I slowly sipped on my cuppa.

Subsequently, I remembered the monk of thirty-nine years of exile, Thich Nhat Hanh, who said that he actually dedicated a whole hour to drinking just one cup of tea. That, in turn, had caused me to become aware of the importance of differentiating others' values from my internal values, since I could not see the relevance of spending one whole hour over a cup of tea. How could he? Then having watched the movie, *Making a Cup of Tea*, I did the maths and concluded that sixty people or more people were directly or indirectly involved in its making. In which case, a minute's tribute for each individual does seem fitting, so that one could take an hour to drink a cup of tea.

With the last sip down my throat, I said, "I must be getting on; wow, is this the time?"

I just had to smile, because I realised that I had actually spent a whole hour drinking that cup of tea. Whose value was it that I had actually used up an hour drinking a cup of tea? Or even to have had the use of the precedents of gratitude that I felt? And I assume that asking, "How could he?" would be just like asking, "How could I?" Do we so easily clown ourselves in roles that give an inclination we are but whole? Mindful-awareness, in this case, had shown me my infantile stage in the game; it seemed a bit like playing chess, which requires commitment, dedication, and attention for success. That is not with the exclusion of the gift of time that is often perceived as Santa Claus' eternal Christmas stockings being filled.

Continuing down memory lane led me further down wandering paths, feeling heavily burdened, as I did the day when I heard the bishop say, "Seek ye first, the kingdom of God, and all its righteousness; and all other things shall be added unto you." Immediately, a seed was planted in me.

Then came the desire, so that when the preacher-woman said, "Cast your burdens upon the Lord," I said, "Yes!"

And when she said, "He will give you all your heart's desires," I said, "Yes please!"

It was right there and then I threw down my sacks of guilty charges, that had felt so heavy, right there upon the Lord. I was slain to the ground, and in fact, that was when I first knew of total acceptance. Over time, I felt heavy again, which was due to all sorts of unanswered questions. It seemed for every unanswered question, I gained myself a conviction that declared me guilty as charged.

Then, I heard the voice as though from the depths of my soul: "Have you ever taken the time to find out exactly where all those guilty charges are coming from?"

"Guess what?" I said. "You may not believe this, but most of those charges were issued by many church brethren, family, and friends, and including other systems of things. You only have to see the look on some of their faces and the way they roll up their eyes; you know what I mean? Furthermore, you should hear how they treat me: "How dare you walk around with no load and not a care in the world, while we walk around with these heavy loads? You lazy thing! Bam! There you are!" And then, I would be issued a hefty conviction of guilty as charged. Of course, I would humbly accept, because we were often being reminded that we ought to bear one another's burdens. That is why I carried the guilty charges of other people, as well. I would get highly praised for being helpful, and so, the more I helped, the more charges I would gain. This may sound peculiar, but they would reward me with even more guilty charges, which they called bonuses. I felt trapped.

Now, since the fashion was the bigger, the better, I soon found myself carrying huge sacks; the mind-weight, to pretend otherwise, was as heavy as the charged themselves. It was a bit like wearing high heels with an annoying pinch to your small toes.

Feeling good heavily depended on the quick turn of supply on demand, which admittedly was never short. Of course, recycling became fashionable, too, and that meant my constant supply was always at hand. I wanted others to know that I also wanted to save the world. After some time, I got fed up with recycling guilty charges, because it meant that I had to find ways of disposing them on others all the time. Some people were happy to have them, and others, well, not so happy. It's just what is called a chain reaction. I think they were often received in the spirit that they were given. Why? If I noticed someone was unhappy to have them, I would take them back and apologise, especially those I found difficult to validate.

My guilty charges had become so accommodating that I was just swiping as though they were real credit cards. In fact, when you think of it, they are perhaps the most real credit cards you can ever find. The trouble is, no one takes the time and energy to go through the terms and conditions, until the creditors are compelled to reveal only the points necessary on which you have broken your contract. How can you argue when you can't even recall signing the contract in the first place? Plus, I had them in every colour you can imagine. It had happened just when I was about to sign the gold platinum; something hit me, as though I was selling my soul. And that's when I became frightened.

Then, I heard the preacher-woman say, "Come to the Lord in fear and trembling, and he will free you from all your burdens." Well, I only needed to get more frightened until I trembled, and that's when I went before the Lord. I was slain, again. It was as though I had a petite mal seizure. Actually, I found out that is a really wonderful way to rest from any heavy load, because getting older generates a wish to travel light. Once you have shared your load, you just feel lighter.

And I like the fact no one gets a chance to see your knickers, because you get covered up quite quickly. As for feeling shame, that simply does not exist in this game.

And you never have to feel bad for not being able to carry your load, because Christ bears our load. If you feel guilty, just remember, someone had helped him carry his own load.

Remembering is good
And even enlightening too!

Then, I got another charge for off-loading on the voice.

I mean, you know what it feels like when someone offloads on you or even when you feel regretful that you've just offloaded on someone, which leaves you saying, "Phew! What was that all about?"

So I would continue to answer the altar calls, ensuring that each time, I was filled with fear and trembling. I mean, getting slain felt so nice; you open your eyes and forget that you couldn't once bear to look in the eyes staring down on you. I would be rendered the wonderful gift of lightness, the feeling that I would get each time I had dropped my burdens upon the Lord. Consequently, somehow, that high like my LSDs began weighing quite low on the scale onconscience, which is claimed to be responsible for responding to the altar calls whilst trying to establish equilibrium, in a light sphere. I just felt that I could not keep treating the Lord as though he were a washroom; not that he ever complained, but nevertheless.

Then I was reminded by the Praise and Worship Team that we acknowledge the Lord in singing and dancing, with harps and with tumbrels and instruments of ten strings. I must say that they weren't stringent on specifics, but I thought, *This is right up my street!* The feeling of arms swaying so high had left me convinced that all these instruments must have their biological parallels right there in me, which had to be their manifestation in the physical realm. You should have seen the way I was moved to my feet, with tears rolling down my cheeks.

It seemed somewhat like manic depression, with my extreme highs before the Lord and, then, the extreme lows of the need to unburden myself of sacks of guilty charges. It had become a sort of addiction. If you ask me, it just didn't feel right. It was like being back in Auntie Lyle's shop getting my fix: a smile, and to be left with the feeling "I just want to hide." On reflection, I saw that guilt is just simply two-faced. You get a smile, but it leaves you feeling sad inside, until your next fix. Stands the reason, I felt that perhaps the bishop has got a point, after all.

It seemed as though I had made every decision based on my emotions. Therefore:

I affirmed that I … will endeavour
To have my guilty charges DROPPED, therefore
I will allow myself to imagine
That I am feeling and breathing light.
I am walking light on this journey.
As a result, I will pay attention to see
How best I can, indeed, end this addiction
And get onto the Bridge of Actualising Self-full Love.
Since like attracts like, I would get a high.

I realised that one of my strengths was my swiftness in using the resources available to me, so that was why I often prayed and sometimes laughed as though I were insane. So I often reminisced on aspects of my life with the intention that it could serve me well. It is with this understanding that I say

Remembering is good,
Though painful at times, but good!

After attributing a moment of stillness on Wondering Path, I remembered it was said that "if you are feeling laden with guilt, it is because you are doing something against your conscience." The audible and familiar voice rang quite clear to my ears. The law of attraction was responding to my concerns: the sermon from the pulpit that day was "Let your conscience be your guide."

Now, I was still faced with the question of the use of conscience, which had been my comforter for the longest while; my axle and my scale; and my perimeter for morality and for attempting to get things right. Regardless the case, I loved the idea of having a conscience that would save me of shame and embarrassment. It also gave me a sense of belonging, and perhaps that was what I liked best. It was so, not only when I had behaved as expected and went with the flow, but even when I had behaved unacceptably, by going against the grain, so to speak. My conscience gave me a sense of empowerment and responsibility, too. Empowerment in the sense of believing in myself as a co-creator. As for responsibility, though a defiant sinner with LSD, I valued the fact that I had been entrusted by the maker to handle such a phenomenal tool: One that could break or make or even amend the rules. Though unaware at the time, using my conscience made me feel special. I was a miniature God, actually making judgements of others: *Certainly, these people can't have a conscience, behaving the way they do; if they did, they'd be like me, and surely, the world would be a better place.* This, I would think to myself. A conscience, no doubt, I came to question its validity, especially with trying to understand why I continued to get things wrong and felt guilty as charged.

Perhaps I have overlooked something, I thought. In a sort of a strange way, I felt that I needed my conscience to guide me, to examine itself, even then. Was it the scale, or was it the product of guilt that was being weighed?

Remembering is good;
Painful at times, but good. This, I told myself.

As I pondered on the emotion responsible for me getting things wrong, I realised that guilt had been the forbidden tree from which all bad fruits fell. There, I recognised that my garden was indeed my conscience.

In short, I had broken some laws. No, not really, because it was the same guilty feeling that I had experienced even as a child, like when I had stolen a biscuit or told a white lie. Like when it was said to me, "If you love me, you would ..." and of course, reluctantly, depending on the impact of the guilty charges, I'd oblige. No matter how I looked at guilt on the scale of conscience, the feeling was the same, like everything else; it just grew bigger over time.

Now, it seems to me that we tend to perceive conscience built on the assumption that a behaviour is right or wrong, based on its outcome. That is, whether one has created the dung effect on the scale of his conscience, which is often determined by others' proper or improper use of their scale of conscience. This is generally done on the basis of the sensitivity and consideration that one feels the other ought to express. Thus, we would hinge on the premise that guilt really equals that one has advertently or inadvertently committed a sin, either against herself or someone else and God. Consequently, the individual concludes such an act had been performed against her conscience. Perhaps the real question that one should be concerned with is, Whose conscience is it, anyway?

Now, coming from a Christian background, this teaching of guilt was entrenched in me and impacted on my decisions and, most profoundly, around sexual relationships. It seemed that the two greatest crimes at the time were sexual relations outside wedlock and murder. While the former impacted on me, in a somewhat muddled way, the latter, no doubt, seemed easier, because nobody took the slightest notice of people who say, "I'll kill you." Then, I felt guilty that I was using words or acting in ways that gained little or no attention whatsoever.

Sexual intercourse, when unmarried, was different and laid the sin, fornication. Subsequently, though destructively, I felt a degree of self-empowerment, even in my disempowerment to ask, "Whose conscience is it, anyway? Who determines that I should be handed guilty charges for my sexual activities and call them sin?" And sin, as we have learned, is the downfall of man, through Adam and Eve's disobedience to God. The couple had eaten of the fruit of the Tree of Good and Evil, which was planted in the middle of the Garden of Eden, even though they were commanded by God to not eat of it. That was man's first sin. However, I later learnt that that sin had also been construed as Eve having "done it"; I mean, she had intercourse with Lucifer, who enticed her to eat of the fruit. Now I often felt, had it not been for either of these cases, we'd all be saints right now, instead of being born sinners. Consequently, because of this primary and secondary learning, I felt I had gone against God's will and was sinning all the time.

Just like Adam and Eve, because they were ashamed after being found out by God, went into hiding and covered themselves, so it was also my need to cover up my guilty charges. This feeling followed me religiously up until I was the age of twenty-eight and was due to be married. Then, I told myself, *Now, I can have God wipe my slate clean! I can repent by asking him for forgiveness of my sins.* However, the break-up of that marriage meant I continued to sin, of course, though I felt that I was consciously trying not to exceed the "seventy times seven" mark for forgiveness. Presumably, according to some Christians, this indicates the countless times we should forgive others. *If only I could forgive this much, God would easily forgive me,* I told myself. No doubt, I have been found guilty as charged for missing the mark.

Remembering is good!

Painful at times, but good to be back from memory lane.

It was a feeling like you've gone way past your limit on your credit cards and exhausted all your financial resources on all sides. I felt weighed down with guilty charges, which included the separation of that marriage. In addition were the teachings of the Holy Bible: that what God has joined together, let no man put asunder. Consequently, I gained more guilty charges for initiating our separation. In no time, my slate was becoming full again.

An affair with a married man felt like double-adultery, and that taught me a huge lesson: that my slate had become immensely stretchable and had facilitated records of over ten years of this particular type of sin, including others of different context.

The charges seemed like they'd never stop, nor would they be dropped. Now I didn't know that one could actually incur interest rates on guilty charges, but there it was, with increased rates. You see, in the tough class of the Open University of Life, I was taught that once divorced, I could remarry under the law of the land. However, I had been indoctrinated by certain Christian beliefs that to remarry was not considered real; only the first husband counts. On the other hand, they said, "If your first husband was dead, then ..." Ah! This teaching had caused me to worm my mind on the next big crime but had found me guilty, even before really considering the crime.

The old saying "Where there is a will, there is a way" had proven true. I got married again, but I struggled to convince myself that I was no longer living in sin.

Now, this is where I totally agree that it is absolutely not wise to always make decisions based on your feelings; that is, of course, if our reasonings can ever be absent of our feelings. On the other hand, it could be perceived that it is such feelings, even that of LSDs, that bear the seeds for change, in the first place. However, the challenge would be whether you can develop enough sense even in a confused state to make a healthy decision.

A further bout of guilt had almost crippled me, so that I had instigated another separation, and the lessons were being presented yet a second time. I felt challenged by my understanding that both sins and joys evolved around sex. Therefore, unbeknown at the time, confusion had become the focus for my resolution. Letting my conscience guide me had proven futile, in my "saintly" attempts to abstain from sin, which left me wondering, What exactly is the issue? Is it the charges or the conscience or an inability to really weigh right?

Remembering is good!
Painful, at times. Sometimes good, sometimes bad.

Often when I had gotten slain, it felt like I had an implant, and my conscience would work quite well for a while. I remembered the people I had hurt. I felt lightened by simply saying "I am sorry." That was working out so well for me that I would even say sorry to the people who had hurt me. You see, I was taught from the teaching of Christ, that before you go to the altar, if you have an issue with another person, to leave your prayers at the altar and make your wrong right with him or her. Consequently, it seemed as though I was saying sorry to everyone, until one day I heard myself saying, "Excuse me for breathing."

It was at this point I knew something was clearly not weighing right on my scale of equilibrium.

This certainly was not what I intended to attract in my life. Either the scale had a default or I really did not know how to weigh right. The maths was not adding up. There was no substantial reason why I should have to endure constant charges and need to dispose of them. I had obviously made some wrong choices, but should that mean the end of me ever having a chance to experience a guiltless and harmonious relationship with another? It was as though I had been tricked by God. He gives me choices and puts all these conditions in my way. He knows very well that I cannot meet them, which raises the question, Whose conscience am I operating under, anyway? Furthermore, it seemed to me that is exactly the same game God played on Adam and Eve. Is this not what is termed manipulation? (no, I mean, *Godi-pulation*), I wondered.

I mean to say, "You put the Tree of Knowledge of Good and Evil in the middle of a lovely garden, where its focus cannot be avoided. You make the garden the home of one that you created and commanded him not to eat of the Tree of Knowledge, and don't touch it. Later, you created a beautiful female companion for him. They are given liberty over every fruit and herb of the garden. You also offer a serpent as a present to them (which they could fllip around). How do they know that they know what you really know … that the Tree of Knowledge is indeed Good and Evil? Is it not inevitable that the tree would become the centre of attraction, given the fact that you have *drawn* their attention to it? I can only conclude that perhaps, there was a very significant purpose, yet to be discovered, from this Godi-pulation notion of human disposition to sin.

Understandably so, the premise that we are all sinners, born of Adam and Eve, in my view, was a call for resentment of making me a born sinner. Of course, I could not resent God! But what exactly did I do? Like self-hatred, I resented Eve, which meant, I was again pronounced guilty as charged. The fact that I openly admitted this truth, perceived by some as blasphemous, I was again found guilty as charged.

Now, in my secondary school of life, I hated Adam, too, because I didn't want to seem unfair; therefore, I just had to tally up the scale of equilibrium with him. I just never understood why people were telling the story over and over, with such unfairness, as though it weren't a big deal at all. They claimed that it was all Eve's fault, and that was despite the fact that the command of the forbidden fruit was directly given to Adam and not Eve. Furthermore, in deciphering the essence of this teaching, I had not been able to wrap my head around the fact that Adam and Eve got punished. Though understandable that it was consequential, for every action there is a reaction, nevertheless, I thought that God's judgement was rather steep on Eve: the pain of childbearing, which experientially had served as a further reminder by which I was charged.

However, in today's world, I am presuming that it would seem *conscientiously* justifiable to ask God, "Why did you find it necessary to plant the tree in the middle of the garden? Furthermore, have you forgotten that you made me in your *own* image and likeness, with a predisposition to sin and to choose?" Was it anything like this, then? No! Instead, when asked by God, "Where are you?" Adam took no responsibility to mindfully answer the question. Instead, he said, "I heard your voice in the garden, and I was afraid, because I was *naked*: I hid myself." He could have simply said, "Here am I, Lord God" (or however else he referred to God).

"Who told you this truth that you have discovered?" God asked him.

There, we get the impression that Adam became defensive and blamed Eve, when he replied, "It is the woman that you gave me."

Now, Eve accepted the "lame blame" but ended up dropping it like a hot potato onto the serpent. As far as Eve was concerned, the serpent had enticed her with assuring words: "You shall not surely die."

I don't recall God asking the serpent any questions. However, had it been asked of him, why ... or any other question, for that matter, the serpent might have answered:
"

You see, the fact that you made Adam and Eve in your *own* image and likeness, I can't take the blame here. Though I thought, when you said, 'Let us make man in *our* own image and likeness' that you were referring to me also. As a result, I did find something in me, by which I could find something like myself in Eve, to which I could attach myself to, even as the means to communicate so effectively and share this beautiful garden, of course. Furthermore, how would they learn that you had indeed created them in your own image and likeness? How would they learn that this likeness that you are has in itself, good and evil; they are simply two sides of the same coin? And by being and expressing their true nature, they are now able to identify a force as good as you and me, too, of course.

I mean to say, all the guy did was simply use his "freedom pass" to explore the blessing that you disposed upon him. Remember what you said? "Behold, I have given you *every* herb bearing seed, which is upon the face of the earth, and *every* tree, in which is the fruit of a tree *yielding* seed: to you it shall be for meat."

Now bear in mind, that was before their point of signing, I mean sinning. How would they know that the process of achieving such a blessing to be fruitful, multiply, replenish, and subdue the earth means the actual process of cultivation for transformation? Could they have dominion, as given to them, otherwise? If they never know what it means to die or even lie? And perhaps, they would learn the end of an existence whilst moving into another realm. To make matters worse, you poured down that heavy rainfall, with the weeds growing so rapidly, and you had no one to till the ground. Now you've got Adam sweating enough for cultivating the whole ground.

So whose conscience is being questioned, anyway?

As I continued this investigation, I began feeling better and a lot lighter, too. The argument was making sense. *Who am I?* I thought, making such observation of an argument between God and the serpent. Of course, that nearly gained me a guilty charge. However, I stood my ground, as I continued to observe the unfolding of a Luciferian world, because, like Eve, I believe I shall not surely die. So the argument still had Lucifer to carry on:

"Furthermore, you must have known from the moment there was *Eve, ever*ything evil would live: thus showing both sides of the coin of life. Notice, what happened once you breathed into man's nostrils and he became a living soul? Evil literally, became the flip side of live. Subsequently, the expansion of breath had made everything in-Eve-a-table, as sounds that have been concealed in the word 'breathed' by which you gave man life.. Now, let me tell you what happened to Adam:

He heard her breathe.
He eared ahead.
He heard her heartbeat
A-thread, he had tread the heath;
Her heart had bear a red tear;
He had bead her, that he'd be better.
He had a bed: the earth.
He ate the dread herb.
He retard at three.
He had a bet, dat death be the debt.
He bathed the head, there
He ate the bread, deter-ed the tea;
The tree at the heath had bear a thread.
And all she said: "Here-are!
Dear hearted dead?
He art beta read the breeth!
Er he be de-breathed.

Now, if you ask, all this sounds real to me. Unless, of course, you want to *de*-breath them, by which, of course, a breath must go round, full circle; otherwise, it would not be whole. And if it's not whole, it's not a breath; you know that". *Rightly so*, I thought. That's exactly why, at that stage, God just dwelt with the consequences, by casting the serpent onto the ground; presumably, an eternal sign for interfering.

Nevertheless, the seed had been planted. The legacy of the blame game of guilty charges had now been established, which was initiated by the couple's reciprocity. Behold, Adam had become the perfect subject. He had found something in himself in which to attach himself to Eve. The shared act of acceptance of one's disposition onto another meant that the guilty charge had gone round full circle and had weighed too heavy on the scale called conscience.

Memory lane had led me to the Garden of Eden, where I was faced with the original sin. I saw that the result of seeking wholeness presented the urge to dispose of guilty charges, on all points of the scale of equilibrium. This happens, especially, when one feels cornered. Thus, by avoiding taking responsibility for their actions, it births a guilty charge that somehow is not just two but becomes four-phased.

Firstly, I could see that while serving in Aunty Lyle's shop, I had consented into accepting the seed of what the other had disposed on me as law. That law had mirrored to me a wall with the slogan all over it: "can't even weigh right" or "don't even know how to weigh," and I internalised it, just like the cup of tea that had taken an hour to drink. Secondly, that crime had created in me a feeling of inadequacy that I should not be in the position that I was, serving at the counter. Therefore, I was often feeling a need to buy my way in. Thirdly, once I had allowed the customer the surplus, to defend my position, I was subconsciously easing myself toward the attainment of a guilty charge by engaging in covert agreement of exchange: a guilty charge for a smile. Lastly, once the goal had been achieved, I would feel that I had really broken a law.

On close examination, I discovered that guilt had been deceitfully sold to me as "Buy one and get three free." Guilt had hit the four-pointer axle of my conscience. I mean, all the customer did was give me a smile, but it had the ripple effect of running the whole nine miles. I had allowed myself to be lied to.

Now I can't help but think that my case somehow explained exactly what had happened to Adam and Eve. They had broken the law that served as a wall, which contradicted their liberty to use their freedom pass, at large. Their exploration, nevertheless, would have seemed necessary to develop their perception of the garden and themselves, thus their boundaries. Perhaps that is what guilty charges are meant to do: Like child's play, one discovers the composition of LSD. In turn, such actions would support the idea that God's intention for the Tree of Knowledge of Good and Evil was for man. Where there is man, so too is knowledge of good and evil; just flip sides of the same coin.

Now, since the sense of wrong was established, likewise was the call to do right; thus drawing on the need for perfect balance on the scale of conscience. But whose conscience are we talking about? Was their punishment determined by the crime or a projection of God's conscience for putting the Tree of Knowledge of Good and Evil in the midst of the garden? Perhaps the answer lies in the dichotomy of using up an hour to drink a cup of tea. Moreover, God's avoidance to ask the serpent any questions at all reflected the demarcation that *knowledge* of good and evil had indeed gone round full circle amongst the four entities: Adam, Eve, the serpent, and God.

God's spirit of discipline would prove vital for understanding what replenishing, multiplying, and being fruitful entails. We see that every significant act of creation lays a checkpoint for another step of life's dance. It's a dance that offers us insights to the way we actually develop awareness of God's true nature within us, which is sharing. When we take time to look, we are able to see that sharing is not only projective, it forms the common denominator throughout all of life's events; thus, I was able to see how I collected heaps of guilty charges.

Therefore, it would seem inevitable, on this basis, that for Adam to have accomplished the first commandment: to be fruitful, mutiply, replenish the earth, and subdue it have dominion..., he would need to break the second commandment: to not eat of the Tree of Knowledge of Good and Evil. That in itself would seem the only means by which to continue to activate the seeds of what it means to have dominion.

I get the distinct impression that the two commands were interrelated, like life and death, good and bad are dependent one on the other. In other words, it would serve as the simple maths that where there is one, there is also two; without first, there is no second; and so on.

CONCLUSION

My investigation down memory lane certainly opens a window of understanding of the inherent intertwinement of internal versus external. The displacement or perception of those values is what, in turn, becomes our guilty charges. Take, for instance, Adam's response to God after having eaten the fruit; it had the semblance of guilt all over it. At that point, I am not sure whether it was God or Adam who found something like themselves in the other, but the two connected, anyway. And it seems like God could only have met with Adam where they both were, in the garden, through a game of hide-and-seek.

Had Adam's response to God been something like, "I am here just savouring the lovely experience that I just had with Eve, and guess what? It was, like you would say, very good." Things might have been entirely different.

A common reason why we blame others is due to the absence of remembering, and this might have been the case with the guilty couple. It seemed that they had forgotten to remember the all-inclusive offer God had made. And for God, to say to Adam, "Do not eat of it," does seem contradictory (unless, God was testing the memory capacity). Perhaps the memory system had been underdeveloped and the recall button had a defect. I mean, Adam did not remind God of the first gift that followed the first command, which was "Behold, I have given you *every* herb bearing seed, which is upon the face of all the earth, and *every* herb; to you it shall be for meat." So it would seem like we were also blessed or/and cursed with the seed of forgetfulness; and like wise the seed of memory.

Now I am near my checkpoint of this investigation, and I can't help but wonder, what if there was a great conspiracy of a Godipulation notion, that Eve should have taken the blame for being too smart? I can see how everything would work out just perfectly. Just like my return to memory lane seemed to be working out just perfectly, so that I could now follow the first commandment. I had forgotten to remember, a condition which stemmed from the idea that God had forgotten to remember the first offer he made to man, and Adam had forgotten to remember that the command of the forbidden fruit was given to him and not Eve. However, Eve played smart, because she knew that with God, she could be nothing else but good. Eve saw her name had reflected in *Ever*ything that God created. And she knew that God saw *ever*ything that he had created as good. Hence, the serpent too can be seen as a good present that helps to show the endless breadth of possibilities. Due to this revelation, I had to be mindful not to come out of this investigation like a cracked topped cake.

Now isn't this really Hope for the People?

I can only conclude that evil can be as good as good, unless one chooses to make it bad.

Now, maybe Adam happened to just stumble on his surname, and the others felt guilty for pulling such a joke like that and decided to keep it a secret. Perhaps, this might have been the seed of secrets; after all, they must have had their seed somewhere. Either way, guilt's not so bad, to have awakened such a wonderful discovery.

I think the reason Adam was sent to cultivate the ground was so he could *ev*entually figure it out by remembering to forget his guilty charges. Then, he could awaken to the fact that *he*, too, is in "*Ever*ything." He would see, like God, whether what he had reacted to was being good or bad.

The final analysis is the realisation that the formation of guilty charges derives from a shared idea and shared conscience. Therefore, to subdue our emotions, as an example, we are able to exert control with logic to gauge the balance to weigh right. All this is not in the absence of feeling, even in it's passive state of numbness.

I also discovered that while law can seem to be the cause of my trouble, it is also the means by which I understand my potential freedom to excel and venture. Law as a wall, for any reason, is simply an erection set as a goal, by which one reacts to get self-actualised: It must fall down to get realised. Now, the focus on feeling and outcome of my actions is really my game; especially since the scales of equilibrium have been embedded in my brain. Thus, I am feeling so light in knowing that the distinction of my internal and external values is simply a dance of the law of attraction: the law for life's equillibrium.

"I realized that I had created this condition
(of forgetting to remember)
And, I am now willing to release the patterns
In my consciousness that is responsible for this Condition."
– Helen Schucman, *A Course in Miracles*

RECOMMENDATIONS

Enrolling in any school of life demonstrates your condition: You have forgotten to remember rather than remembered to forget. To revert this condition often requires a visit down memory lane. Therefore, let your first lesson be to remember your chosen subject and to always be thankful for the witnesses' comments and gestures. As a result, let them serve as confirmation for the attendance of your intention to remember to forget. Make it a good seed, because in essence, they have performed a good deed.

From there on, you will know what to do; where to go; who to connect with; and you will have attained your desire, which inevitably involves the interplay of your internal and external values, often packaged as guilt, with the choice to flip into freedom. It may feel like a forty-year journey to get to where you want, but the important thing is to remember, the Crimson Light abides in you forever.

Like a well-risen cake, just cooling before I can be served,

Case closed!

Now, that's what I call a Godi-pulation notion; the gift of choice to abandon all guilty charges to actualising self-full love.

Anchoring Points

There are no accidents and no coincidences, but the choices
we make: Today, I am making a choice to have
balance,
truth, and
awareness.

I am now open and receptive to the guidance of the Crimson
Light; therefore, I am trusting the choice I have made to be
light,
guiltless, and
free.

The Rear View

How is my driving?
I ask myself as I ventured into the past;
As though responding to every potential hazard of my journey,
I am reversing to the scene of the crime.
To find the lessons from another angle,
That could further help me
Get onto the Bridge of Actualising Self-Full Love.

CHAPTER SEVEN

The Rear View

Perhaps the unconventional exit of Mr. Barack Altidore, which bore the emblem of death, had got me thinking of my own exit from Grazebrook Primary School. The same force had now beckoned me to still take a good look in the rear-view mirror. As a result, I continued to immerse in thoughts of life and death, even beyond the passing of Mother. By that, I was able to explore my primary learning in the school of life of funerals on the island of St. Lucia. Perhaps this smoky black hole would altogether share its side of light.

Usually, on the first news of a person's passing, you'd hear people asking, "Who die? Who die there; who they say that die, uh?" And by the time you heard a second round of the news, you would know they could not have been referring to the same person: Since you would be answering, "How is me, uh?" Because your name had been pronounced as dead. Thankfully, we have more reliable information, such as the television obituaries which include a eulogy of the deceased.

Traditionally, villagers would assemble at the dwellings of the deceased for the wake. They would meet at night and brew spiced teas and coco tea thickened with white flour, to which small dumplings would sometimes be added. The local ground coffee was guaranteed stimuli for keeping the people awake. In addition, it was always a perfect opportunity for the woman with the peanut basket to earn some cash. The men would play dominoes whilst drinking shots of white rum in its unadulterated form. I never understood why the men would repeatedly indulge in a substance that caused their faces to repel, like a wrung washcloth hung on lines or even dried prunes. Their "ahhhhh" expression would convey the clear message that they had successfully managed to take the 90 proof white rum down their gullet, often without coughing.

Crying and lamenting at various intervals would not get in the way of the usual storytelling and jokes, often about the deceased. Ensuring to catch everyone's attention, the storyteller would begin, "*Messiè krik krak!*" or "*Tim Tim Bios Sec!*" To this day, I use the phrases as indicating an unbelievable story is about to be told. This would continue night after night until the body was laid in the ground. The eve of the funeral would be coated with the solemnity and anticipation of the day most dreaded for the mourners. And with the excitement of women chit-chatting whilst arranging flowers, it was also the message of a sleepless night.

As a young child who lived near the church, I often got caught up in the funeral processions which would end up in the nearby cemetery. Now, as in olden days, there you had queens of professional and novice mourners, ensuring for a perfect grand finale. You didn't have to know the deceased, but you did what the Bible says: "laugh with those who are laughing and mourn with those who are mourning." In retrospect, I would say that I was taking my training in both modules quite seriously.

It would be impossible to think of funerals without considering the grave-digger and the fisherman, Lazarus. The two always seemed like an odd combination, in my view. I suppose it was a matter of convenience, since he not only lived near the sea, but also quite near the burial grounds. You could easily tell by the vigour with which Lazarus applied himself that he took great pride in covering up the grave. Some said it was so because he would know exactly where to dig when he returned, since he had other dealings with the dead.

Lazarus was regarded as good looking; his reputation, however, was considered bad, dark, and ugly. Despite that, he often seemed unperturbed by the rumors that the thick books he often read were evil. Evidently, Lazarus cherished his books; he was even willing to risk his life to save them. He had to be held back from the blazing flames that had burnt his wooden house down to the ground. Living near the seaside, the wind had proven much too strong for the villagers, who carried buckets of water in an attempt to save the house. That day, Lazarus had earned himself many caring and compassionate friends.

As a friend of Grandmother, Lazarus showed his loyalty by paying her frequent visits, sometimes twice a day. Due to his reputation, I would often tell him to go away, calling him a *Maji Nwe*. It was an accusation that he would have supernatural sex with women whilst they were asleep.

"You want to make sure that you see their faces the next morning; yes! Well, don't think you are coming here tonight!" Lazarus would laugh in my face and would behave as if we were friends.

On at least two occasions, he admitted to me that there was not one human vice on earth that he couldn't do. He also said people think that the Bible is used only for good, but it can be used equally for evil. I now understand the saying "innocence is bliss." I am thankful that I was too young to know the extent of the vices that he meant. All I knew for sure was that I was too busy to take Lazarus serious in any way whatsoever. Instead, I learnt to deal with my potential fear, by looking at the biggest feet I ever saw. Otherwise, I could end up feeling quite intimidated by the six-foot-plus giant. Then I would quickly put up my guard by developing a tough exterior, in the exchange of words that conveyed "You do not frighten me." He might have been Goliath, but I was the David who would slay him with my words.

Even though I would still remember that it was said that he dealt with the dead, I would say, "To hell with you!" The Crimson Light on the Sabbath would shield me, and I'd be safe.

On the other hand, I had secretly developed a great deal of respect for Lazarus. He was a man who openly demonstrated not only his feet, which he referred to as the Ten Commandments, but also his faith. His lifestyle gave the impression that he did not seek the public's approval. Oh, how I looked forward to watching him pass by on his way to church.

Lazarus, a Christian of Seventh Day Adventist doctrine, would get all dressed up most Saturdays in collar and tie, but often, there would be no shoes on his size twenty-plus feet. Keeping the Sabbath holy meant I could tease him as much as I liked, even though that meant that I was breaking the Sabbath, by my inappropriate behaviour.

I sensed that my grandma loved the fact that I stood up to Lazarus. In hindsight, I could only conclude that perhaps she was scared of him. I was never reprimanded for speaking to him harshly, and so my confidence and cheekiness just grew stronger and stronger towards the grave-digger. I think it is safe to assume that since Grandma was always preparing for her death, she might have preferred to think that the likely grave-digger would be covering her in a somewhat graceful manner. It was equally hard to exclude Grandma in my reflections of how people deal with issues of death on the island. And being Lazarus' friend, I cannot exclude Grandma from this equation.

It was hard pleasing Grandmother, and I think that's why she took control of planning her death and her funeral. It felt like a ritual in the quiet way she'd say, "Take the dress that's in the trunk for me."

"Which trunk, Nan?" I always asked.

"The big one underneath the bed." Both were always underneath the bed.

I would pull out the white-turned-yellow dress, protected by mothballs and garlic cloves. "This is the dress I will get buried in when I die."

Perhaps the smell was to induce death, because on three occasions, Grandma had gotten the priest to grant her Last Rites. And I remember that he bluntly refused her a fourth, after which she went on to live over ten years.

My hardest job ever was trying to please Grandma.

Like Mr. All-Bags-Full, it was either too much or not enough sugar in the tea, or too much or not enough salt in the cooking; it was the same for any other ingredient that was used for consumption. It was through Grandma I gained my scholarship into the tough primary and secondary school of life. With Grandma, everything was, "Beat her! What that girl needs is a good beating! She is too rude!"

Now, could I really feel sorry for Grandma when she had trouble walking and was immobile? My compassion tank had become permanently low and was in need of topping up; therefore, where Grandma was concerned, I constantly operated on reserve. It had remained so until I eventually plucked up enough courage to invite Grandma to one of my therapy sessions.

One of my challenges was coping with Grandma's prejudices. Generally, she made no bones about her preference of colour, even though she was quite dark in complexion. She seemed to lean to people of fair complexion and those who had become associated with city life or who stood for something in society. Those were the attributes for one's nose being raised, so to speak.

In retrospect, I realised that my reason for describing a visit from my two cousins as being from hell had stemmed from my resentment of Nan's preferences. They had come to visit us from the neighbouring island of Barbados. At the time, I seemed to have found an outlet for my cruel intention of making another pay for my unhappiness. I had picked on the one I felt was prettier and fairer than I was, a behaviour I have deeply regretted over time. Thankfully, the Crimson Light had been kind to foster the opportunity to write off this ordeal and offer a sort of equilibrium for both of us.

I had longed to be recognised and valued by Grandmother; that would have helped to tip my scale of empathy towards her. Instead, I just could not get past the series of trials and tribulations. For instance, an unhappy expression on my face for having to dip my hands into a bag of coals first thing in the morning would slap an identity card on my forehead. She would say, *"Yich bouick! Yich towo! Tèt wed!"* ("You are a child of a mule! A child of a bull! Your head is so hard!") All that did not help. A little love like what Uncle Richard's children were getting, whenever they came on their weekend visits from the city, would help. They looked well-polished and were also well-spoken. Their mother seemed mixed race, but I didn't know the difference at the time and thought she was just like the priest. I had gotten the impression that "whiter" meant brighter, in all senses of the word. They did not seem to ask permission to smile or laugh as they ran around. I, on the other hand, felt as though I needed permission to breathe in Grandma's presence. In turn, I also felt that this kind of treatment seemed to have allowed others to treat me like a maid, instead of family.

I had to endure Grandma's drilling in my eardrums: "Make sure there is fresh water for when they come! Open the cabinet, make sure the glasses are clean, and make sure you don't break them! Sweep the yard! Hurry up with the food; they will be hungry when they come. After all that time, you haven't finished washing the clothes, and you call that washing? Time to come and comb my hair." Now that was something I looked forward to, because I always enjoyed combing Grandma's hair. Apart from the fact she had the loveliest, softest white cotton hair I ever saw, that request always warmed me up inside Perhaps, it was the stories that she related or the opportunity to get close to her. Nevertheless, in my heart, there were lots of things I liked about Grandma: She spoke very good English, unlike Mr. All-Bags-Full; she could read and write very well. Combing her hair gave me the opportunity to hear the stories, time and time again.

The most popular one was about the explorer who went to Marlborough and met a lot of foolish people on his way. He made a bet that he'd marry the first, a beautiful young lady he had observed carrying an empty basket on her head. A few yards from her home, she would take it off her head and set it down on the ground. She watched it for a while and then put it back on her head, and once inside, she would tip it upside down.

"What are you doing?" he asked.

"I am collecting sunlight to dry out the floor," she replied.

"Well, young lady, I will say this: If I ever find another as foolish as you, I will return and marry you."

On his arrival, Marlborough seemed like a ghost-town with no one around, and he wondered where everyone could be. So he headed to the church steeple to utter a prayer for what he had dreaded. As he drew nearer, there was a great noise of people, with ropes tied all around the church, and they were pulling in all directions.

"What seems to be the matter?" he asked.

"Well, we have a grave problem! A dog has pooped right at the church entrance, and we are now trying to move the church away from it."

Without question, he quickly found his treasure, and the explorer returned to honour his word by marrying his foolish bride. He had not learned that he could have broken his word, but then again, like attracts like.

I had not fully extracted the essence of the story, but the way in which Grandma told it always made me laugh. In retrospect, I discovered that I could also cause others to laugh, by telling Grandma's stories.

By the time Grandma had finished my long to-do list, in preparation for the loved ones' arrival, it would be said that my lips had been touching the floor, and that I knew was indeed a fat lie, for the floor would certainly be wet.

Speaking of lies, I do admit that there was a time when I was not quite sure what was truth and what was a lie: Due to the fact that Grandma had persuaded Aunty Lyle to give me the biggest beating ever. I felt that I was going to die, and so I lied and said that the false report for the beating was in fact true, and she stopped.

As far as I can recall, it was my first and only beating from Aunty Lyle.

That, in turn, had completely ruined the usual excitement and anticipation I used to have for Auntie Lyle's fortnightly visits. Despite the many gifts from her, the whole beating thing had left me on edge. Consequently, it had been a challenge trying to figure out what responses to give people, especially Grandma. One could say that during my time under her supervision, I had gained a distinction in my course of knowing how to lie. Consequently, even that proved futile for my scholarship of higher education in the school of life.

I often enjoyed waking up after I had fully satisfied my palate on the aroma of fresh coffee being prepared by the neighbour who lived three houses down the road from us. It was sort of my alarm clock at four thirty, though I often wished it were later.

There were other stimuli, too, like the crowing of roosters and the exchange of morning greetings amongst farmers and fishermen. It would be a contrast to the evening tiresomeness. The boisterous sounds of children echoing from various directions meant the full awakening of the village. It was a mix of laughter and mourns and grumbles about completing their chores, before going to school. Like fetching fresh water from the public cistern, going to buy bread, combing their younger sisters' hair, and attending to their animals and so on, interweaved with the latest news: "Who they say that die, uh? Who you say?" And a eulogy would be taking place right there on the sidewalk.

But the main early risers of the village were people with no private lavatories, the treasure dumpers. They were usually up about four o'clock. It would still be a little dark outside; that was, apart from the monthly full moonlight, which would light up the whole sky. The dumpers were all hoping that no one would see them with their treasure pots in their hands, whilst others had their pails on their heads. Although it was a practice by many of the villagers, you could sense that there was also a degree of embarrassment of people feeling exposed, in an undignified way. It was more like a horror movie. People walked past each other as though they were all sleepwalking and not uttering a word, like a ritual. However, it would not be kept silent who the participants of this ritual were, once an argument had escalated into a quarrel.

For whatever the reason, I failed to take account of why some days the alarm clock would not go off. That meant I overslept and would be rudely interrupted by patrons who would come to buy coals, because they had not prepared the night before for the morning's breakfast. As the salesperson, I was responsible for serving charcoals or whatever else was on sale at any given moment. There was always a lot more than charcoals on sale. Whatever the arrangements between Grandma and the farmers were, the produce was often left there as though our home was a warehouse. Since Grandma was disabled, I felt as though I had no choice in the matter, in terms of my role. However, I did on occasion exercise my right: an insight of the Crimson Light to actualising self-acknowledgement. I would refuse to get up by the early knock on the door. I'd just pretend not to hear them, especially if I did not have Grandma's treasure pot to deal with that day.

The way I saw it, I did what I felt was expected of me, but my main job was to figure out how to meet others' expectations. Of course, some things I learnt much quicker than others. For example, I quickly learnt to wake up early enough so that I would not be spotted again with Grandma's treasure pot on my head. I quickly learnt to rinse out the laundry well; otherwise, the sun would leave yellow marks on the clothes, which would cause it to look most unclean. Moreover, it would save me from having to wash them a second time. Nevertheless, the process was never smooth sailing. Notwithstanding, I gained some badges of mainly unpleasant stereotypical labels, from family and friends, including my neighbours and peers. That was enough to substantiate my identity as rude, slow, strong-headed, and lazy, all in acknowledgement of my presence.

With my two best friends in my frontal lobe, Resignation and Chatterbox, I would retreat under the cedar tree: my secret hiding place by the sea. Surrounded by an abundance of pink petals, I would daydream and forget my pain. I would dream of another place far, far away, with no buildings. It would be my own secret garden. The lawn, well-manicured, surrounded by flowers, was never seen before. I would be there on my own, and all to myself, I would dream.

Other times, I would hide behind the activity of eating, just to take a peep into dreamland. I was not always successful, because of the announcement, "Hurry up, dare, to wash the wares!"

I will disappear and never have to come back, I'd tell myself. Even though it was a rear view of reality, to me at the time, it helped me validate my escape into dreamland.

"Why is everyone calling me rude, stubborn, and hard-headed? Why they calling me names and saying bad things about me?" Then I would feel compelled to examine myself because they also said that the sores on my legs had gone way up. Why should I keep drinking that Epson salt mixed with sea water when it's not making me better?

In fact, it was through my constant morning dips in the ocean in hope of healing that I discovered the cedar tree. I suppose the scratching from the irritation of mosquitoes and sand flies did not help either. I thought, *Why everything is me?* I had not provoked the insects; I felt that even they hated me too. I had done the maths that tallied "People were just like mosquitoes and sand flies; they're either attacking me or sounding really awful in my ears."

I'll go far away! Yes, one day I'll go far, far away, I told myself. That made "far away" my favourite two words of any story.

Sometimes, I would lose myself so far in dreamland, and Resignation would say, "Okay, I suppose you could just stay there, because they don't really want you here, anyway." I had taken this to believing that he meant "here on earth." Then I would say, perhaps things might change one day, since I had Chatterbox to entertain me with songs like "If I Had Wings I Would Fly."

Now, I had gathered the report of my childhood experience with Grandma in the village of Micoud and made some wonderful discoveries, such as the fact, I can make people laugh by telling her story. It obviously meant that I laughed with Grandma more than I had realised. I also had the opportunity to appreciate her fine qualities, including many visits to dreamland, by which I have now been able to develop a good sense of imagination for the Bridge of Actualising Self-full Love.

Going down Grave-land Port with Lazarus felt, to some extent, like walking through the corridors of death itself. Although I had been the David who had slain Goliath, Lazarus, I was only now acknowledging my fear. Nevertheless, I valued the experience to try and make sense of one of life's eventualities, even that of Mr. Altidore, who had stepped into the tombed casket, just like that.

However, I also became aware that somehow, something or someone had placed a note with a map on my mental dashboard that read, "Remember! The wonderful place that you often saw in dreamland, it really does exist. You only need to be mindful of your journey, and you will recognise it." Then, I began to feel like when you have missed your exit off the highway. It seems to take forever to return, just to get back on track.

Looking for landmarks you might have passed, that had caused you to become even more alert, whereby you become more conscious of using, and in some cases losing, all your senses. As you look in your rear-view mirror, back and forth, left and right, you listen, not only to the sounds that you might have registered on the way, but also to your heart to guide you. You even remember the feeling you experienced when you saw a certain tree or flower, all to aid you back on course. You wonder, "How far is it before I can exit?" But then you hear the voice of someone screaming out your name, and with a smile, you slow down to say, "Hello! How nice of you to remember me."

"I can't forget you; you use to be the coal-merchant girl who lived with your grandmother on Lady Mico Street.'

"Nice to see you too."

"And you had lots of sore on your legs too. You still look the same; you haven't changed, uh."

Okay, as if I didn't know, I would think.

Vroom! Vroom! Byeeeeeee.

I would not hang around much longer, because I could tell exactly where this was leading: "You were also her treasure dumper."

And right there, I understood the beauty of being your own chauffeur in life. I realised that I could just move on. The Crimson Light had offered me the choice to accept what I had heard and seen. Even the rear-view mirror had served as a reminder of the experiences that fuelled my journey to the Bridge of Actualising Self-full Love. On the other hand, would I allow the fear of such comments to drag me down and make the choice to go somewhere far away from who I really am? Calling out my name had been no accident, but an opportunity to discover why I was there, and to remember I am:

One who is stemmed strong like the cedar tree,
With branches way high that touch the sky,
Accommodating clusters of pink blooming flowers
And ready to provide others in need, a safe place to hide.

Hence, I realised that I had literally been grounded and
rooted in my favourite words:"Far, far away." This is not in
terms of geographical distance, or even feeling emotionally
removed, but rather, it is the inner calling to see the world
and all its beauty in all life's journeyas one giant cedar tree:
How can I tell you the real beauty of the cedar tree?
The tree that felt my pain and anxiety
And had beckoned me unto itself,

Spilled around, laid arrays of fresh sweet fragrant flowers,
That willed my footsteps; as I picked them up one by one
And raised each, to my nose, until I had
found myself next to its trunk.
No! Not smooth, but to this day, excites the palms of my hands
With sensations that let me know, indeed, I am not on my own.

The crack of its bark no doubt reflects my pain;
Yet, its strength reassures me, "Oh no, you are not insane."
I can't resist, I break a piece of the sweet scented bark,
That permeates my senses until it sedates me,
Then I gently slide and cradle myself between its roots
That look like Grandma's breasts,
Where I can enjoy the feeling of its immovable peace within.

Through this rear view, I now realise
That the cedar tree has provided many with houses
And tables, under which children, too, would often hide,
All because they gave carpenters' pencils to make their marks
That the whole world not only rowed in boats to far distant shores

But many travelled far, far away, whilst they sat on benches,
Even in their own homes, and others sat on stones.
They learned not only how to read, but also to write.

I was blessed to see the unearthed, pruned
branches of the cedar tree
Consumed by fire; bleak and black, it had matched my own pain,
Yet packed in bags that Grandma and I had sold.

Could I ever count the number of meals that they provided?
Or the bellies that were filled by delicious meals that they cooked?
All because the cedar tree always provides a safe haven
That continues to grant us satisfaction.
Even when we are ready to be laid in the tomb,
An ascension by which we vaporise the sweet scented flowers.

Until then, may the blackness that cured my pain
Sill provide others emotional ease that they, too, would know
What it means to be black, even like coals.

I had to decide on one of several exits at the roundabout. To avoid the tendency of becoming anxious about missing my turn, I went round the circle a second time. At that point, I became aware of others waiting and wanting to be in the circle. I saw that there were still lessons to be learned. Most important was the fact that by going in circles, and not taking an exit, I not only hindered my progress but also that of others. In which case, like my friend Julian would say, moving in the same circles means I had taken on the position of an enemy of progress. I saw the importance of moving with purpose You not only progress but you also inspire others to do likewise; and to trust that the Crimson Light, like the cedar tree, always provides, protects, and prevails.

Then, I remembered that I had observed the burning incense stick of cedar that had sent forth its smoke in all directions. From there on, I knew that I could anchor on a book or a meal, for in true essence, the cedar tree exists far, far away from any enemy of progress. Thus, one may wonder what the relation is between the bright pink petals and black coals that Nan and I sold. They are both rooted from the same ground, on which the Crimson Light never ceases to shine. In a roundabout way, the coals help us meet all our basic needs for life, whilst the flowers reflect the beauty of the light from within. Therefore, it is important to develop the confidence that no matter how bleak or black your circumstance, and like my witness of Mr. Altidore's descent, you are never really alone. For as you keep moving in the world, the strong woody scent of the cedar tree calls you to follow its trails, where you can bathe your soul in pink petals, as though they were fine gold.

That meant it was time to change my lane as I sang, "Nearer my Bridge to thee." I had noticed an array of blooming cedar trees along the way. The Crimson Light had alerted my attention to absorb the wonderful sight, by which I saw that far, far away had also been deeply rooted in me. The cedar had found something like it in me, by which I was led through the rear-view of going back, even in circles, where I discovered my inner resources that propels me forward, to the Bridge of Actualising Self-full Love.

Point of Anchor:

There are no accidents and no coincidences, but the
choices we make: today I am making a choice to
dream,
touch, and
live.

I am now open and receptive to the guidance of the Crimson
Light; therefore, I am trusting the choice I have made to
appreciate,
understand, and
expand.

CHAPTER EIGHT

The Combination of Actualising Self-full Love

There was a temptation to give up on the knock that banged on my heart's door, but once more, I am compelled to be open and press forward, with determination, to succeed in my quest. After all, Mr. Barack Altidore would have had to do the same to achieve his goal. Although not formally appointed, I became aware that he had been my mentor. He descended into the smoky black hole while I, on the other hand, yearned to ascend. Therefore, I believed that the principles he applied mattered and were the flip side of the same coin.

Just like the coupling of the glow and the warm reception of the dogs outside GPS had proven enough to sustain me, so was the marriage of my vision with determination, to keep my spirit ignited. However, even determination requires sustenance. I was forced to conclude that, whilst I felt I was progressing quite well, the weariness seemed like a hot midday journey, like climbing the island's Morne Kengea; with no shade at all, one finds an inner juice to continue to the top. With the need for a boding place to anchor for a while, and just to be still, I carried on.

I can boldly take my refuge in Hope for the People, I thought. *The Crimson Light will protect me, and I won't be in need of that mortuary, not just yet.* As I quietly uttered these words, I got a sense that I was rising from my own tomb and disembarking on the Bridge of

Actualising Self-full Love. My path, however, still seemed like an eternal black hole. Perhaps it always gets worse before it gets better, in which I keep my faith, it must, and will, get better.

Though faint, it was important to collate my thoughts and have them in some sort of organised manner. Set principles of order had re-emerged before I could relax. The process of thought-filing generated a feeling to celebrate the advent of all that I had achieved so far. *They seem like wonderful trophies*, I thought. *Perhaps they really are trophies I had gathered along the way.*

With each step I made, a sheet of light extended beneath my feet, and on banners on either side, I saw the words "the allegiance of the Crimson Light." The journey through smoky hills and valleys was providing me a checklist. It was time to take stock and combine my resources for my staying power, so I could make it to the Bridge of Actualising Self-full Love.

I saw it was good that the allegiance of the Crimson Light had never failed to show the extent by which a little question – "Why am I here?" – had rippled in my life, like throwing a pebble into a pond. Regardless, my spells of confusion were also the provision of the beauty of the cornfield in my mind. I had learned that everything happens through the choices we make and are constituents of cause and effect. Thus, we are able to shape our situations by the meaning we impress upon a thing. With the value and insight that such a question would evoke the answers I was seeking, I joyously crowned my head with my first trophy.

I saw that my desire for the Crimson Light was good for my dance of the quickstep tango, but I also developed an appreciation for the benefits of tiresomeness. I was forced to slow down and retreat into stillness. There, I was given the chance to assess the vision and mission necessary to achieve my goal, and through my own global positioning system, all I had to do was observe whether my companions were helping or hindering my progress. I had tuned into the right frequency, with determination to succeed in my quest. For instance, I had found the strength to stand up for myself, even against my endurance of Mr. All-Bags-Full's treasure pail. I had tapped into the vision to experience the sweetness of my sleep. For this reason, I proudly placed my second trophy in my brain.

The Crimson Light, through the darkness of Mr. Altidore's smoky hole, prompted me to examine what I had left simmering on the back burner. It not only saved me from my potential unrecognizable disasters but provided me the opportunities to speak up for myself, such as learning how to ask for help, like I did with Sylvia; that day, we bonded while picking peas. To have such a lovely memory to anchor on, I laughed whilst I place my third trophy in my voice-box.

It was good that I recognised the opportunity to examine the ties that bind. Although I cannot say that I fully understand all its implications, I have gained a degree of insight of the characteristics of the yarns: how they become rooted and form various contours in the fabric of the ties that bind. Therefore, the perception that the yarns equate an indestructible Jericho wall is simply untrue. But it makes me realise, one can never really hide, because walls are indeed destructible. With that awareness, I take delight in knowing that I choose the fabric of my soul by storing my fourth trophy in my heart.

I saw that it was good, that the paradox of the Crimson Light seemed to present the chance to role-play various acts in helping us assimilate what we want to project to the world. But it also allowed me to see, through life and death, what had previously been sketched out in my world as wrong and right, until I found the scale of my own purgatory for balance. Therefore, I played the child, seeking love, so as to continue parenting my child with love. The light had shed rays of wisdom, and by that, I honoured my fifth trophy, as I felt its radiance right in my solar plexus.

Hallelujah! For I saw it was good that I should have no shame or blame, to shout out loud, "Not guilty as charged." The lame game of blame that had proven to be a Godi-pulation notion was designed to only help me find my gain to the Bridge of Actualising Self-full Love. The investigation that I had undertaken led me to have all my guilty charges dropped; it felt quite tedious at times. However, I'm amused by the fact that I now have no reservation in expressing my feelings like a well-risen cake. Therefore, I hope others can not only partake but use the ingredients by which they can create, in the sacredness and according to their specification, one like my sixth trophy as I joyously place it in my pelvic.

I saw it was good that by Mr. Barack Altidore stepping into the tombed casket, just like that, it not only took me to GPS, it also determined my return to the primary school of life, on the island. There, I reunited with my grandma and the grave-digger Lazarus.

Demonstrating his feet as the commandments, Lazarus had liberated me into gaining my conviction and letting go of anything that could prohibit my progression. The grave-digger had shown me what would happen if I did not pursue my goals. I could be like one of those walking-dead; someone could happily throw dirt on me. His act of consistent and forward movements of his feet was also a demonstration of how close he held his values, evident in his every step. That meant he gave himself no choice but to find comfort through his close connection with mother earth. Basically, Lazarus lived by the proverb, "As one, through his desire separating himself, would seek to engage in all wisdom." Subsequently, I felt that it was no accident that Lazarus and Mr. Barack Altidore had showed up in my life. This led me to believe that the two had actually conspired in stirring my life to fulfilling my desire of getting onto the Bridge of Actualising Self-full Love.

Now the fact that Grandma seemed preoccupied with her wedding/burial dress had me wondering that maybe she, too, was simply acting out her role. In hindsight, I can't see what other glue that might have held hers and Lazarus' friendship. What message was she conveying in the reminiscence of her wedding? Was it a day to die for? Yet she went as far as to protect the dress with mothballs and garlic, and she requested that the priest grant her Last Rites. Perhaps the oath "Till death do us part" carries more implications than I had perceived, thereby including children and all others concerned.

I can only assume that Grandma was trying to teach me a very profound lesson, that her dance to preserve life ought to be one of protection, like mothballs that keep mites away and the aroma of garlic that harnesses us onto nutrition for our sustenance. Thus, protection against anything serves as a reflection of its existence, in whatever sphere that may be.

Perhaps Grandma's love for me had excelled beyond the physical realm but was to be found in the everlasting trails of moth balls that kept creatures like cockroaches away and the captivating aroma of garlic, the "must add" ingredient, universally used in everyday cooking. Thus, I have been provided a template for life, though figuratively, I might add. I was given a rear-view mirror from which I not only faced my childhood days on the island, I was pleasantly astounded by the flip side of my early impression of Grandma. With that said, I graciously and whole-heartedly embraced my seventh trophy and placed it firmly at the base of my spine as though it was a golden throne on which I would sit. Like a queen, I will reign.

I was elated by the realisation that I had indeed gained seven trophies, reinforced by the belief that nothing happens by accident, and that the bunch of seven keys had served as a symbol for unlocking the solution that had birthed each trophy. Yet, I still had not reached the Bridge of Actualising Self-full Love. Don't ask me how I knew, but just like I had become aware of the jump in time, once outside GPS, I knew I had not reached the bridge.

The Crimson Light had shined on everything. Hence, I became aware that the dark feeling of needing to accept a position was conveying a message for stillness once more.

Maybe it was due to my unquenched desire to satisfy my appetite of the Crimson Light in GPS, or perhaps the contents of the lost diary, still in my mind, had not permitted the sovereignty of getting onto the Bridge of Actualising Self-full Love. Sometimes, we hold on to things that have ceased to serve any good purpose in our lives. They may not necessarily be bad in themselves, but they can take up time and energy, thereby distorting our attention from what is truly important. For this reason, I would have to return to GPS once more. Maybe it was the six-inch-thick wall that I could not quite figure out, but I felt the need to retrace my steps.

I discovered I had gone to the school my son was attending to collect a report. Only that time, the report that had been written in a diary was about me. Parents and children, including the teachers, were all in high spirits on the sunny summer's day, as though in celebration for the weekend ahead.

"Can I help you?" a woman in black came up to me and asked.

"I am looking for my diary," I replied, and I immediately noticed the clock on the building had showed four o'clock sharp. In hindsight, it was as though she was expecting me. While I felt certain that I had not handled the report, I was still able to read the blue-inked words that were handwritten onto two yellow pages.

The woman in black had offered to get me a new diary, so I followed her down the long hallway and into the basement of GPS. The journey had formed a semicircle, thus leaving a mental impression of a perfect "C" in my head, I suppose, because it matched the one Mr. Promise had given me. So excited, I joyously exclaimed my preference for one of vibrant orange, yellow, and red. Once there, the woman in black directed me to the neat stacks of diaries. My excitement quickly waned at the sight of black diaries, with the exclusion of just two: with black/green and black/red. However, as far as I was concerned, the fact I did not see a diary of my choice did not mean one did not exist; I quickly concluded it was not the right time.

It was just like entering a doctor's surgery; once there, I'd become alright, but I would still wait to be called in. And then, an amazing thing happened. I felt so peaceful and happy there. The environment was most welcoming; I could not want more. The lounge was spacious and felt very light. The man at the reception desk seemed nice; he smiled at me. Before I could relax, I checked my mind whether I could permit myself to indulge in the moment without having to rush back. In response to my concern for my son, I was told he was alright, so I immediately relaxed; it was time. *Peace, love, sweet peace, just where I belong*, I told myself. Gratefully, I welcomed the invitation to sit for a chat with the woman in black. As I recall, it had not been much of a conversation, but more like being together.

Who was the woman in black? She reminded me of Sister Blanchard from the Hephzibah Pentecostal Church I used to attend back in London. Sister Blanchard, who always wore a wig for whatever reason, I don't know, was an Afro Caribbean woman I considered as the mother in the church, who readily nurtured everyone. You'd get scared trying to get close to her, but once you did, you'd be asking yourself, "What was that all about?" The façade would be off.

As I reflected on the woman in black, I saw that the Crimson Light always seem to present someone or some situation to mirror to us our intentions. I had found an amusing distraction, as I thought of Sister Blanchard and her wig. It was always a challenge trying to keep a straight face whenever I was in her presence. My focus would often bypass her eyes and immediately zoomed to the top of her head. I would find the funny side to whatever we were talking about, so as to create an outlet for my laughing at the wig that often appeared upside down or sideways on her head, whilst at the same time uttering a short prayer: *Forgive me, Lord, for what I am about to do.*

On one occasion, I offered to help fix Sister Blanchard's wig. She was so happy that I actually paid attention to her image. She began to relate the story of how one day, the wind had blown her wig right off her head. "It had happened whilst running for the bus," she said.

I eagerly asked, "What did you do?"

She replied, "The bus had stopped, and I could see from a distance where the wig had anchored onto the stem of a tree. For a moment, I was not quite sure what to do. Should I fetch the wig or get on the bus?"

"Well, what did you do?" I asked a second time.

She took a deep breath and said, "After I turned my head left to right, several times, as though I was watching a tennis match, the bus driver's patience had won. I decided to let go, plus getting to work on time was more important. I just got on the bus, bent my head down low, and whispered, 'The Lord is a very present help in time of trouble."

I learnt that prayer instantly; it became a mantle for shortening my forgiveness list.

As I smiled at that reflection, I understood that I was really choosing the rhythm and flow of my journey, and everything was simply a reflection of the choices that I had made. Therefore, I was ready to tune into time, season, and reason in accordance of my objective.

The woman in black (I had not even asked her name) did not wear a wig, but her hair's natural disposition gave the idea that hers could pass as one. She was simple, kind, and gracious and also spoke in a clear and distinct tone, undeniably her own. She was divine and compassionate; she was just nice. I think it was her warm presence that had caused me to sleep on the red couch.

I had slept for exactly one hour before waking up, to find out that I was the only person left in the school building. All the lights were on. My initial reaction was, "Why didn't someone wake me up? They obviously did not do a health and safety check before going home; otherwise, I would have been discovered."

My ego was firing on all cylinders, but not for long. I was distracted by the bright lights all around. I had never seen lights like this before. They were bright crimson, and they conveyed a feeling like the morning sunrise on the east side of the island, and the orange sunset on the west, were actually kissing. It was an astonishing sight. The marvellous rays of pure delight had been enough to just bathe my soul. It was at that point, I also discovered a bunch of keys in my hand, but with the thick wall semi-ajar, they had proven a useless concern for their use.

The only way out had been through the narrow doorway, just wide enough to go through. You see, the door itself was not narrow at all; the six-inch-thick wall that was wedged onto the left side made it seem as though the wall had a mind of its own. It was talking directly to my mind: "Allow me to guide you out." Since I was increasingly becoming aware of how to receive blessings, I humbly accepted. *Weird*, I thought, *when you think you communicate with objects, like a wall.* Perhaps it was the state of submission to the force, since I had subdued my temptation to prolong my admiration for the lights. At which time, I proceeded to make my exit through the wedged door.

Lo and behold, there were the two security dogs outside, opposite the dilapidated pet food warehouse, just standing there and looking at me. Somehow, I could read their minds; they wanted me to acknowledge their loyalty towards me and know that they weren't going to allow any harm near me. They, too, could read my mind, as I conveyed through my eyes a blessing of gratitude, after which they instinctively lowered their heads and left. The dogs, the wall, and I were one, just like Chatterbox, Resignation, and I had been one. I concluded that there had to be a relative field for this oneness; otherwise, how could the wall and the dogs respond to my will? I suppose it was no accident or coincidence; as it's often said, walls have ears.

My anticipation of having to face outside in total darkness was instantly dissolved by the unexpected brightness and presence of the three men: Mr. Altidore, Harry, and Christian. Although surprised, I can't say that I was ecstatic about either the brightness or the men. Perhaps it was due to the fact that I had already programmed my mind and was unafraid to walk through the darkness, even if it had been one o'clock in the morning instead of a little past midnight.

The men were clearly not interested in my immediate query about what I had discovered in the GPS, so I let it go. Yet I was able to decipher, at least, even through the intervals of confusion, that something profound was happening. In my quick summary of seeing Christian, I realised that I was over our break-up, despite the fact that my marriage had proven difficult. I simply acknowledged the fact that Christian was a real gentleman who totally respected me and became aware that all romantic feeling for him was truly gone.

My main focus was about learning to love myself more and getting onto the Bridge of Actualising Self-Full Love. *But what the heck is Christian doing here in St. Lucia, all the way from England, and standing there just like that?* I thought. *Of course, must be to see me! But why pretend otherwise that he would not even acknowledge my greeting?* Well, that was not so difficult to sum up, because Christian just wasn't good at expressing his feelings and would just keep them to himself. He was the type of man whose sentiment was as such: the fact he told you once that he loved you should serve you for the rest of your life. He maintained the view that if there were any changes on his part, he would let me know, but how could there be changes when everything was based on routine? It seemed unfair to wish the death or birth of another, just to break the routine.

In my attempt to communicate my feelings, I once said, "Sweetheart, you don't kiss me as much, anymore."

He replied, "What did you do with the last lot I gave you?" and he'd be serious. Not to mention, he was a man of very few words, so I got tired of throwing my words at him, which just fell on deaf ears, anyway.

I had never before met someone as emotionally and materially detached as Christian.I also concluded that maybe that was what I really admired about him in the first place. He seemed to know how to protect his emotional well-being and always be in full control. *I could learn to do the same one day,* I used to tell myself. I had obviously found it too challenging to get the right balance with Christian. I felt that romantic love, without a great deal of emotional investment, was not possible, and therefore, I would rather follow my truth to actually connect with a man in a profound way. This belief, in itself, had at least provided the perfect environment for complete honesty. It was time to move on.

And now, I believe that it was through our relationship that I learned to walk away from the light when I did that day.

I must now journey on
With my life; on this earth,
In this place, in this sphere.
For now, my work has just begun.

To find out why I am here.
I suppose I am here, because I signed up for a role,
True, I am told, though I had not understood this much,
That to learn and to know,
Whether implicitly or explicitly,
That there is a cost

For my attendance at the Open University of Life,
Had presented me set modules,
And the role foretold is to know that which unfolds,
That to teach, I had to learn,

And to learn, I had to experience,
And to experience required my active participation
Of what subjectively and objectively had become
the derivatives of my awareness.

I saw that by letting go, I gained insight and courage to feel lighter, to go on winning trophies and awards.

Now I have gone in, and I was out again; it was time to take another look at the dilapidated pet warehouse. The dogs, one white and the other black, had conveyed another message, other than being there for my arrival. I was anchoring with determination to the force by which I was able to read the diary and the same force that guided me out. And I got the distinct feeling that I needed to pay closer attention, for by this I would get the full significance of the two dogs. Their contrast was typical of funerals. Perhaps it was meant as a subliminal forewarning of my witness to Mr. Barack Altidore's descent. On the other hand, I had the strong feeling that they were Grandma and dear Lazarus in disguise. Did they wait all this time to see how I would react to my witness of Mr. Altidore stepping into the tombed casket, just like that? I wondered.

As the thought waved in my mind, there was the voice again in my head: *There are no accidents and no coincidences, but the choice that we make.* "They're just dogs," I reminded myself. "No, they're not, they are gods, and that is why it is said that dog is a man's best friend. Have you spelt dog backward"?

Oh my God! Immediately in that moment, I saw everything. I was hearing everything. Yes! I was right that Lazarus and Grandma's friendship was about me. The force of the gods had beckoned me to relive that experience, so that I could see their commitment and love towards me. They had been training me for this journey onto the Bridge of Actualising Self-full Love. Now, I can see that my pursuit of self-full love is actually mirroring a depth of love that I would not have otherwise known. I just had to extend my arms in full surrender to the heaven: "Give me the capacity to embrace this immense goodness," I prayed. I realised that the intensity of Crimson Light had stayed with me as I made my exit, and that was why it was so bright outside; subsequently, it formed a demarcation of the existence of a new era.

I was learning fast; if the clue for the dogs had mirrored God, then it must be that the same principles applied to the faded 'pet-food warehouse' sign. I mentally reversed the words to "house-ware" and "food pet," but that did not feel or sound right. And for what I knew, I would be mistaken to think that the gods would make it that simple. With that conclusion, a big sign, "F for footwear" showed up on my mental board, followed by Lazarus' big feet, just looking at me once more. I thought, *How typical, just typical.* I was faced with the Ten Commandments: It was time to take notes. It was proving a bit trickier than I thought. I tried to associate the remaining words to Grandma. But I must say, I had to smile at God's humour.

The induced stillness caused by the acrobatic juggling of letters into words had tested my determination. Then I saw "Used Hope." "What is the message here?" I asked. Was Grandma telling me that she had used Hope for the People services? Or was it her recognition that I had used hope? This had only felt half-right. Grandma seemed to have softened up, because then, words were just popping up before me: *"He," "Used," "Deep," "Hose," "Pose," "up," "see," "us," "do,"* and *"seed."* They were all words formed from the remaining letters of "Pet Food Warehouse."

Of course, Grandma and Lazarus were both quite literate, I thought. I felt that I was under examination from the gods. What sense am I supposed to make of this? I wondered. Answers didn't seem to prolong, as if I had been programmed:

"He can't hurt me now," I said with conviction. "I used to be afraid, but not anymore. I am no longer affected by the sight of a piece of green hose. I can hold my head up high and feel good about myself. I see the transformation of my pains as gains. It's now easy for me to refer to us as one. I am now mindful of what seed I am planting. With determination, I can do anything I set my mind to do."

Then I paused and remembered how I would pose, trying to disguise the treasure pots for the disposal of its contents. I had gotten stuck on deep, because I felt that the gods were trying to help me understand the combination of the Crimson Light and to actualise self-full love. I accepted the notion that it was necessary that I delve deep. So I saw that whilst I had distorted my footprints by my range of fancy footwear, I was not exempt of the revisitation of the path once travelled.

As I entered the pet food warehouse, I understood the need for its transformation, to make it the dwelling place for the gods, even as it had facilitated the dogs.It would represent what had taken place right there with me. For I also understood the fact that I must value the other as I truly value myself, regardless of my perception of him, which is only an expression of who or what I am being in that moment. Therefore, how can I value the teacher more than the student, the physician more than the patient, the victor more than the loser, the parent more than the child, or the friend more than the foe? Take, for instance, while Lazarus walked around, laying bare the Ten Commandments onto the ground, Grandma, on the other hand, her feet only touched the floor with little sensation, by which she could identify their location. Yet, it is through both that I gained this awareness: Either dogs or gods, coals or petals, life or death, good or evil, they are one and the same; just flip sides of the same coin that forms the structure of the combination of the Crimson Light. The essence is to always be conscious of their roles in your life.

And so, I made a conscious declaration: I Lauviah declare: I love my dog; I love my God; for by both, I continue to be guided, whereby I had been given a glimpse of the Bridge of Actualising Self-full Love.

I invite you to be a companion on the next phase of this journey and to share the joys that I anticipate awaits me. Perhaps, as an observer, you might have gained more than just a glimpse of the Bridge to Actualising Self-full Love.

Remember, there are no accidents or coincidences, but the choices that we make: And that in itself is the grand *Godi-pulation* notion by which one prepares one's throne.

I now anticipate my joy to uphold the throne of the Goddess, Shakti and have my dog beside me on the Bridge of Actualising Self-full Love.

ABOUT THE AUTHOR

Crimey Queen is a middle age back british Writer of Carribean origin, has moved beyond her fears to being baptised into the literary as an Author with this first volume of the Crimson Light: A bridge to Actualising Self-full Love, to fulfilling her long wish to publically express her literary skills, with subjects close to her heart.

Crimey Queen academic background in Counseling and Psychology and Creative Arts and including her love and respect for nature are treasured gifts valued as tools she feels not only serve her in day to day life but paves her life for increasing evolution.

For this reason Crimey Queen bravely illustrates her ability to hangs on a thin thread for balance and risks her own sanity through Lauviah's determination to fulfill her dream of the journey to Actualising Self-full Love.

ABOUT THE BOOK

The Crimson Light: A Bridge to Actualising Self-full Love, is a transformational journey that rests on the premise "nothing happens by chance but by the choices we make."

After witnessing the scene of Mr. Barack Altidore stepping into a tombed casket, Lauviah becomes haunted by the question, Why am I here? Only to be convinced that she must have subconsciously made the decision to be there at the exact moment of it happening. If that was the case, then why would she do a thing like that?

The quest for answers opened up many bright paths of hope, including hills and smoky valleys of emotions, but it often felt like stepping on the thorns of her family's history of sexual, mental, and physical abuse.

Lauviah's main challenge was not only the emblem of fear of each thorn but also to allow herself the sense of worthiness by which she could bathe in the feeling of sweet-scented red rose petals. She needed the tender properties for healing her broken spirit.

Like an alchemist, Lauviah relies on her insightful ability to see things from various angles and finds a wealth of beauty deep inside her that showed up even in bags of coals.

Her journey demonstrates openness and honesty that makes her intentions quite transparent. Her ability to focus, with purpose, takes her beyond the five senses, where she unreservedly acts on her intuitions, dreams, and imaginations in achieving her goals.

The Crimson Light illustrates the benefits of feeling stuck, by which one is allowed the freeview opportunities to intently look in life's huge mirror, to know oneself, and to see what changes to make.

This journey of actualising self-full love reverberates a sacred vow, witnessed by body and mind, where both heart and soul say, "I do," to the Crimson Light.

CPSIA information can be obtained at www.ICGtesting.com
Printed in the USA
BVOW08s0653280916

463369BV00006B/3/P

9 781504 999762